T0099664

Order this book online at www.trafford.com
or email orders@trafford.com

Most Trafford titles are also available at major online book retailers.

© Copyright 2010 William Quayle Jr.
All rights reserved. No part of this publication may be reproduced, stored in a retrieval
system, or transmitted, in any form or by any means, electronic, mechanical, photocopying,
recording, or otherwise, without the written prior permission of the author.

Printed in the United States of America.

ISBN: 978-1-4269-4822-0 (sc)
ISBN: 978-1-4269-4823-7 (e)

Library of Congress Control Number: 2010917307

Trafford rev. 11/17/2010

 www.trafford.com

North America & international
toll-free: 1 888 232 4444 (USA & Canada)
phone: 250 383 6864 ♦ fax: 812 355 4082

MR JACKSON IN WASHINGTON 2015

America under Socialism

William Quayle Jr.

Contents of My Book

The action that caused me to write Mr Jackson in Washington (2015) is the Health Insurance law 2010 fines people for not paying their health insurance. I have asked for premiums for health insurance and I am licensed in Oregon, four years, and in California on and off 34 years.

There is huge difference in the premiums persistency to get a client to pay the health insurance premium than auto insurance. Major medical costs way more than the auto insurance making the persistency lower.

This is fiction set in the year 2015. All the names and places are fictional with the exemption my boyhood friend that lived a few doors away, Stephen Shambach☺. There is much history that really did happen. The reason I used our 7th President that is the first Democrat President is Andrew Jackson. You will see why he should have been our 6th President. If you told Andrew Jackson you can't do that and it attacked his honor chances are he would find a place to challenge a duel to you. He did not take any crap from anyone. He got the name OLE Hickory after the Battle of New Orleans. The name stuck later, and was just as suborn in politics. If he saw you were trying to destroy the United States constitution you're defiantly his enemy. He died from the wounds from his dueling. I find it only fitting his fictional great, great grandson carries the family name and holds the same senate seat that his great , great grandfather held. That is the connection to the State of Tennessee, and if I cause more people to visit the Hermitage in Nashville, Tennessee it is for the better.

There is some very powerful metaphors that will stick in your mind in this story. Hopefully they make you register and vote. I don't mention any names if you read carefully you will know who a metaphor is pointed at! This story started as a screenplay, changed into a book, and can easily be changed back to a screenplay. If your familiar to the Frank Capra's 1939 movie Mr Smith Goes to Washington there are parts of the plot that are similar. Mr Smith Goes to Washington is defiantly a inspiration in writing this story, and the current events of 2010.

I can safely say it is my work though and my creativity, and reputation for spectacle is evident. Please note, I may not have followed senate procedure by the regulations of the senate. If I did you would have a boring story and I agree with the late director Frank Capra "it is a sin to have a boring moment".

Enjoy my story and it take's you a different time when the government is running people's lives. Let's all hope it does not come to that.

You will find my writing is direct and to the point. I added my screenplay action adventure "Iago's Victory" so you get more "bang" for your buck.

I do suggest you listen to certain types of music to get in the mood they are through out this story.

***

"No one is perfect concerning the low resolution pics.
The important thing is that the message gets across."

***

**August 24th 1814 the British burned Washington. A reminder that
you should never take for granted our 2nd amendment rights to the constitution.**

Prologue

The Twilight zone opening that we all hope never happens

"News bulletin, John and Kitty Kadiddlehopper are sent to the federal interment camp for not paying their government health insurance", says the KPOW announcer.

John Kadiddlehopper and his wife Kitty are 100 miles away from the closest desert town Micaville, Nevada. They are in a federal internment camp that is nick named "poverty central". It is a horrible place for the nation that hides it's poor. Twenty thousand plus live in buildings without windows. If they escaped they be at least 150 miles from any water. The train that delivers new residents has no windows. Bats fly through the open bay buildings that are like barracks; through the cracks scorpions and tarantulas creep in from the desert, and are found on resident's walls. It is like the bats, scorpions and tarantulas are the sins of the American government against it's people. There is only a curtain between residents of "poverty central", and you can hear a pin drop and hear it at the other end of the, open bay, buildings. John and Kitty have to do responsibility therapy, that is slave labor for which that they only make $1.25 a hour. When they get paid for working 80 hours it's not a happy moment; it is a attack on their self esteem. There is no recreation in this internment camp. All John and Kitty have is each other this proves to be a time their love for each other; their marriage prevails and they survive because of it. This is just the tip of the iceberg for not paying their government mandated health insurance. The events that put them in this horrible place is a American federal government under socialism that is gone too far and running everyone's life. The crumbling American families has caused reliance on the federal government to pick up the pieces where the traditional structured family values are getting a thing of the past. John and Kitty's children have been put by court order in a foster home. The Federal Government by legislation has split up a perfectly good family. Senator Jackson in Washington gets wind from John Kadiddlehopper writing him and vows to repeal or roll back the taxes, health insurance law, that put them in the internment camp. The national press is proactive toward John and Kitty and in result national demonstrations are seen in Washington that are the biggest ever seen before.

While this is happening Senator Jackson is putting on a most historic filibuster to free John and Kitty. The protests are so loud you can hear them when the Senate doors are opened.

After the British Burned down Washington August 24 1814.
They attacked New Orleans January 8 1815. Andrew Jackson ,(OLD HICKORY), with
partisans from several southern states used their second amendment rights to bear arms.

Chapter One

From Normal life to IRS Arrest

This is a story about a middle class family That are experiencing American socialism that has taken hold of the country. The Kadiddlehopper Family John and Kitty that are in their early fortes. The they have three children Arnold and Beatrice are fraternal twins at age sixteen. Billy is age fourteen. They have a early American house, with a lush green lawn, in Riverdale, Tennessee. They own one of the two gas stations Riverdale and make about sixty thousand a year.

One spring morning Billy is in the refrigerator looking for the orange juice. "Mom where is the orange juice?" asks Billy.

"Its on the top shelf," says Kitty

The family is sitting at the breakfast table. They are watching the national news on TV that they watch every morning. Beatrice brings in the mail.

"Here is the mail mom," says Beatrice.

"It's a letter from the bank, and the IRS John," replies Kitty

" I wonder what the IRS wants" says her husband, John as he opens the mail? "We were supposed to pay our government health insurance last Friday," said John. He shows the notice to Kitty.

"We pay federal Property tax, higher income tax, AND a 10% tax on our gas station.   How do they expect us to pay $800 on our health insurance? They are threatening to arrest us for not paying or health insurance or pay a twenty thousand dollar fine or one year internment camp," says Kitty.

" Such coercion making us criminals for not paying our health insurance is wrong; we can only pay so much. The government is out of touch with reality. We are in a boat with holes and we are bailing as fast as we can," said John. "As much as we make and it's still not enough we work 24/7," complains Kitty.

John reads the letter from the bank.

"Oh that's just great! The bank in one month is going to foreclose on us!" yells John.

Kitty takes the notice and reads it.

"They might as well feed us to the welfare sharks," replies Kitty.

"It is all the government programs we are paying for; WE are the little fish that feed those sharks. The problem is there is not enough of us that work to pay all the governments social programs. They drove all the health insurance companies out of business in Tennessee by taxing them to death ,or they chose just to not sell it. So we are being forced to pay some high government health insurance premium that we can not afford," complains John.

"Our agent, Allan Raiderson would never ask that of us or force us to pay" says Kitty.

"I am off to school mom and dad," yells Beatrice.

" Have fun cheerleader at practice," says John.

"You have a game against North?" replies Kitty.

"YES MOM, GO RHS!" cheers Beatrice.

"Bye Mom, Dad!" Yells on the way out Arnold and Billy.

"Have fun at soccer practice," replies Kitty.

"We give you this special report At the Hermitage in Nashville, Tennessee. Senator Andrew Jackson V," reporting the YOUCAN announcer on TV

"There has never been such more grave situation as the middle class is being taxed to its limits. For some people it is a total disaster. Thomas Paine said "these are the times that test ones soul" For good honest working people they are being tested. Welfare roles are at a all time high with less people working. Citizens that work, have heavy taxes for some households that are at the breaking point.

I am sure if Andrew Jackson was alive dealing with today's crisis with the federal deficit, make the crisis with the United States Bank seem like a picnic.

For presidential elections I am for only using the popular vote to elect presidents. This subject goes back to my great, great grandfather lost a election in the house of Representatives and had the popular vote. Every year he was president he advocated a amendment to the 12th amendment of the constitution.

The Second amendment to the constitution is also being tested. My great, great grandfather if he could not raise a army of partisans the battle of New Orleans would have been much different. Let me remind people that Washington was burned down before the battle of New Orleans by the British.

Government intervention into peoples lives has never been so prevalent than it has now. I urge every citizen to write to me if your have been trampled upon by the federal government," says Senator Jackson on TV.

"We are being bulldozed by the federal government," remarks John.

"More like put into a hole and then buried alive," replies Kitty.

" It is a blessing that we have Senator Jackson in Washington representing us, he has my vote," responds John.

"The little people have a ray hope. Senator Jackson brings some common sense to the people. We have to get going to the gas station and it best we both go. I did not like the looks of that IRS notice," says Kitty.

"It is best we make plans just in case," replies John.

They both walk to the van to go to work. They drive a few blocks and see a boy riding his bike crossing paths with him, and have to stop John puts his head out of the window.

" Hi Mr and Mrs. K!" yells boy on bike.

"Next Time look," replies John yelling at boy on the bike.

They drive on to work and come to stop light and see two choppers stop next to them. Motorcyclist gives a thumbs up.

"Mr. K!" yelling motorcyclist.

"So who do you suggest look after the kids?" asks Kitty.

"Well we are fortunate that we have a few choices; My brother Billy will do a good job," responds John.

"There is my sister Alice," says Kitty.

"Your sister lives in Kentucky, the kids would have to be taken out of school," replies John..

"Well you ask your brother if they come and get us?" concerned says Kitty.

"I will call him at the station. What make me so upset we are in this fix for just falling behind in our bills," says John.

"We have each other that they can never take away from us," replies Kitty in a sexy voice.

Kitty kisses and hugs John, one romantic kiss.

"Now you call your brother. I will open up the station," said Kitty. John goes to the phone to call his brother in the office.

"Good morning Billy," says John on the phone.

"What is up Brother?" replies Uncle Billy.

"It's the IRS notice we got in the mail," says John.

"So how can I help?" says Uncle Billy.

"The IRS has threatened Kitty and myself to arrest us for not paying our government health insurance," complains John.

"That should never happen," says Uncle Billy.

"The IRS notice said ether today or tomorrow. Kitty and myself were wondering if you would watch the kids if that happens," says John

"Sure Brother and spend time with my god son no problem. I will come by the house and take them to my place if that happens," says Uncle Billy.

"Both Kitty and myself sure appreciate it," replies John.

"Billy agreed to watch the kids if the IRS comes to arrest us," says John to Kitty.

"That's great, (sound ding, ding), We have customers!" yells Kitty.

$10 gas on #7 Said the First customer. "Ten on number seven", said first customer, and pays kitty.

" $15 on #10 and this chocolate" implies second customer.

"$15 on ten and two dollars for the chocolate," says Kitty.

Then a man in a black trench coat. suit, and hat come to the counter where Kitty is working. With him was a Deputy Marshall, he is Deputy Marshall Scully. The officer knew Kitty and John from he bought coffee and donuts from them every morning.

"I am looking for John and Kitty Kadiddlehopper," says the IRS Agent.

" I am Kitty, John there are some people here to see us," says Kitty she yells to John in office and John comes out.

"Yes, who is it?" replies John.

"I am agent Krackenscull and this Deputy Marshall Scully,".

They show ID'S,

"Do you have your health insurance premium of $800?" says Agent Krackenscull.

"No we do not Sir, and I do not see how we can pay it ether," replies John.

"Then I have a federal warrant to arrest you and your wife Kitty. Deputy Marshall Scully Arrest them," says agent Krackenskull

"Please Turn," says Deputy Marshall Scully, as he handcuffs both of them and leads them to sit in the patrol car he gets the keys from John for the station finds the close sign puts it up and closes the door and locks it. He goes back to the car and they drive to the jail.

"Deputy Scully can we pass by 644 Oak to notify my brother we have been arrested," implies John?

"I am not suppose to do that for you, It's on the way, I guess it would not hurt. In my opinion this should not be happening to you two, I am just doing my job. I have to give you your Miranda Rights," says deputy Marshall Scully.

"We Understand Deputy Marshall Scully, it's the federal government not you," says Kitty.

1. You have the right to remain silent.
2. Anything you say can be used against you in a court of law.
3. You have the right to have an attorney present now and during any future questioning.

If you cannot afford an attorney, one will be appointed to you free of charge if you wish," says Deputy Marshall Scully

"We understand, my brothers house is the third house on the right," implies John.

Deputy Marshall Scully drives up to Billy's driveway and gets out of the car he knocks on the door Billy sees Deputy Marshall Scully. Without saying a word

"I understand what I must do, I will get the children," replies Uncle Billy.

Little did Deputy Scully know that letting Billy know John and Kitty have been arrested. It was like telling Paul Revere the British were coming, one by land two is by sea. Billy did not just go get the children; he spread the word that John and Kitty have been arrested for not paying there health insurance

"I need to talk to the KPOW day reporter," says Uncle Billy on the phone; he waits for the day reporter to get on the line

"Can I help you?" says the KPOW receptionist.

"Do you have time to do a very important Report? John And Kitty that own the gas station on 621 Main Street, have been arrested by the IRS, for not paying their health insurance," says Uncle Billy.

" Oh how horrible, we are interested in covering that story," replies the KPOW reporter.

"Then meet me at their gas station, 621 Main Street," says Uncle Billy.

"The soonest we can be there is 3 PM," replies the reporter.

"I will see you at 3PM," says Uncle Billy.

He calls the Riverdale Horizon Press (RHP)

"I like to talk to a reporter," says Uncle Billy.

"I will connect you," replies the Riverdale Horizon Press receptionist.

"News Desk," says News Desk.

"Are you interested in covering a story John and Kitty that owns the gas station on 621 Main Street; they were arrested for not paying their government health insurance," says Uncle Billy

"We passed by there, we were wondering, why they were closed. We are interested in covering that story," says the News Desk.

"Can You be at the gas station at 4 PM?" asks Uncle Billy.

"We will have someone there at 4 PM. John and Kitty they are outstanding citizens of our community, they deserve the attention," says the News Desk.

Uncle Billy then went to John and Kitty's house to get their children and took them to meet the KPOW reporter at the gas station.

Uncle Billy Knocks on the door and Arnold lets Uncle Billy in.

"Arnold, Beatrice and Billy something happen to your parents this morning," says Uncle Billy.

"Let me guess, they got arrested by the IRS," replies Beatrice.

"You are right dear, and I have been instructed to take you all to my house, and we have to meet a reporter at the gas station," says Uncle Billy. They all go to the car to go to meet the KPOW Reporter. while Uncle Billy is driving. "Uncle Billy when are we going to see mom and dad home?" asks Billy.

"Billy, they may be gone for a year," replies Uncle Billy.

" Mom and dad never hurt anyone, or stole from anyone. All they were trying to do pay the bills," remarks Billy.

4

"It is good you all understand what is happening," says Uncle Billy

"I am worried when we get older. Are we going to be treated the same as mom and dad," says Beatrice?

"Best to take one day at a time. You have a opportunity when we see the press. You are the future of America dear," says Uncle Billy.

They drive on to the station looks like KPOW is here in force. They get out of the car.

"Are you the man that called us," implies the KPOW reporter?

"Yes I am, I am John's brother Billy Kadiddlehopper, This is Arnold, Beatrice, and Billy," said Uncle Billy.

"It is good to meet you all now we will start the interview. Billy when did you know John and Kitty were arrested by the IRS?" implies the KPOW Reporter.

"John called me there is a chance they may be arrested. I was asked to watch the children if they got arrested. The Deputy Marshall walked up to my door and I instantly knew what to do, about 11 AM," says Uncle Billy.

"Arnold what do think about your mom and dad being arrested," asks the KPOW reporter?

"Mom and dad never hurt anyone. It should never have happen," says Arnold.

Beatrice in tears, "I just want my mom and dad home again. When we are older, is the Federal government going to do the same to us?" cries Beatrice.

"Billy what do think?" asks the KPOW reporter.

" I think The Federal government went too far today, and something has to be done about it. I do not vote yet, after this I will sure will so my voice is herd," replies Billy.

"There you have it, the IRS Arrested John And Kitty Kadiddlehopper today for not paying there government health insurance. If this the new American Socialism we have seen a bad sample of it today. Freedom took one step backwards. Wake up America! Billy you will see it on tonight's news, we must be on our way, thank you Billy," reports the KPOW reporter.

"You are welcome," to the KPOW Reporter says Uncle Billy . "The other reporter is here, hi," says Uncle Billy.

"Are you the man that called us?" says the RHS reporter.

"Yes I am, I am Billy Kadiddlehopper and this is Arnold, Beatrice and Billy," said Uncle Billy.

"So Uncle Billy what is your reaction to John and Kitty being Arrested by the IRS?" asks the RHS reporter.

"It should never have happened. The federal government is too intrusive. Evidence of that is what happen to John and Kitty today" says Uncle Billy

"Arnold what do you thin," asks the RHS reporter?

"When they put the health insurance law in effect; the law makers did not think they could break up perfectly good families enforcing the law," asks Arnold.

"Beatrice what do you think?" asks the RHS reporter.

"Is this what I have to look forward to when I am older? I hope that is not the case; I just want mom and dad home!" cries Beatrice.

"Billy what do you think about your mom and dad being arrested by the IRS?" asks the RHS reporter.

"Total lack of foresight on the federal governments part. I just want mom and dad home," said Billy.

" We Are done here Billy; look for article in tomorrow mornings news," says the Riverdale Horizon Press Reporter.

"We will be looking forward to it," "We have to get going for dinner," suggests Uncle Billy. They all get into the car and drive to Uncle Billy's place.

"What are we having?" asks Arnold in van.

"How does Pizza sound?" replies Uncle Billy.

"Sounds Great!" remarks Beatrice

"I'm fine with pizza!" says Arnold.

"Me Too!" says Billy They go to the take and bake pizza place get two large pizzas then go home. That night they are watching the KPOW nightly news on TV.

"We are on the news!" remarks Billy.

They all watched the news then went to bed.

Chapter Two

The Court case and internment camp arrival.

The next morning the word got out that John and Kitty were Arrested by the IRS; on the RHP the front page read "**John and Kitty Arrested by the IRS**". At the courthouse the word got around like the shot that was heard around the world at the Battle of Lexington and Concord. People from all walks of life in Riverdale are demonstrators with signs, "Free John And Kitty", and ,"It should never have Happened". With patriotic music the people were having their say. Freedom has taken a hit and the people in Riverdale, Tennessee are reacting to what happened to John and Kitty.

John and Kitty are dressed in the jail dress orange, and are shackled. In the court house John and Kitty are in a meeting with their public defender Alice Rutherford. "I advise you to plead Not guilty and least give you a small chance to be acquitted. The way the law is written it give you very little chance of being acquitted," remarks Alice.

" All we ask of you is you do your very best for us," remarks John

" Do you have someone to look after the children," implies Alice?

"Yes my brother in law Billy we made sure they are taken care of even before
we were arrested," says Kitty.

"Then temporarily we are OK for now. We go before a judge at eleven this morning, There is no trial under the health insurance law the way it is written," says Alice.

"That is just great, they did not read that part of the law when they voted for it," complains John.

" They probably worked out a deal to over look that part about us having a trial," says Kitty

"There is another matter that has to be settled," says Alice

"What is that," implies Kitty?

"The suitability of Billy Kaddidehopper to act as temporary guardian for your children," replies Alice.

"There may be a problem with that because Billy has had a drinking problem. He has been clean and sober for a few years," says John.

"We may see the court have your children sent to a foster home while your in the federal internment camp," implies Alice

"Let's hope that does not happen!" says very upset John.

 Kitty gets John's attention and kisses John.

"There is one thing dear they can't take away from us I love you," Kitty in a sexy voice to John.

"Your so right dear we will get through this in spite what the IRS takes away from us, and I love you too," replies John.

" It is time for us to go to the courtroom," says Alice smiling.

As they walk down the long hall way all the doors are the same, unless you have been there many times like Alice, she knows exactly which courtroom to go to.

They experience that long walk and fear of what is going to happen next is evident in John and Kitty's faces.

The entrance to the court room the press photographers are out in force.

The court room is packed almost everyone that know John and Kitty in Riverdale is in attendance. John, Kitty and Alice enter the court room and Arnold, Beatrice, and Billy meet their parents. They have not seen them since the morning they left for school; before John and Kitty were arrested.

"Are you all right mom and dad," cries Beatrice, she gives a warm hugs?

"People should not be treated like this," says Arnold hugs his mom and dad.

" We will triumph over this no matter what!" Billy hugs his mom and dad.

"We will get through this Brother," Uncle Billy shakes hands and give hugs.

"We must get seated court will be in session any minute," implies Alice.

John, Kitty and Alice get seated at the defendants desk.

" All rise the honorable Jacob Smith presiding, court is in session," bailiff announcing to the court.

Judge Smith looks at the schedule of cases. We have John and Kitty Kaddidehopper verses the Untied States Government. How do you plead," says Judge Smith?

Alice stands.

"We plead **NOT GUITY** your Honor!" says Alice in a assertive voice.

"Mr Ankleus do you have any witnesses," says Judge Smith to the federal prosecuting attorney.

" Yes your Honor I like to call IRS agent Krackenscull to the stand," says Mr Ankleus.

Mr Krackenscull takes the stand end and is sworn in by the bailiff.

"Mr Krackenscull when you asked John Kaddidehopper if he had the money for his government health insurance what did he say to you," asked Mr. Ankleus.

"He said he does not have it, and won't have it as long he has to pay the high taxes imposed upon him. Then I ordered Deputy Marshal Scully to take them into custody," replies agent Krackenscull.

"That is all you may step down now agent Krackenscull. I would like to call

Deputy Marshall Scully to the stand," Mr. Ankleus announces to the court.

Agent Krackenscull steps down then Deputy Marshall Skully takes the stand.

"Deputy Marshall Skully do you concur what agent Krakenskull said about the defendant?" asks Mr Anklus.

"Yes I do. then I did arrest them; they did not resist me," responded Deputy Marshall Skully.

" That is all you may step down; the prosecution rests," says Mr. Ankleus.

"The defense calls John Kaddidehopper to the stand," Alice announces to the court.

John takes the stand and the gallery is in a uproar.

"ORDER, ORDER in the Court!" yells Judge Smith

The court is silent again, but you can see the anger in the gallery faces.

John takes the stand.

"What brought on you and Kitty not being able to pay your government health insurance?" asks Alice

"Too many income taxes, a federal property tax, taxes on our business, the insurance companies not wanting to offer health insurance because they too are being taxed heavily. No one else to buy health insurance from than the government; the government health insurance is eight hundred dollars a month. Then we had to stop paying our health insurance and here we are in a hearing for not paying our health insurance," replied John.

"Under the circumstances something had to give I understand why you had to quit paying your health insurance; the problem is that the federal government does not realize that people have other bills like paying taxes," says Alice.

"It can happen to anyone!" Yells out a voice in the gallery

" It should never have happened!" says another in the gallery.

"Order, Order in the court!" yells Judge Smith.

"You may step down John; the defense calls Kitty Kaddidehopper," says Alice

Kitty takes the stand.

"Kitty what is your reaction to being arrested by the IRS?" asks Alice.

"We are experiencing a federal government that is out of touch with it's people. Our freedom is under attack and the people must send a message to our government that they better start listening to the people. I urge to every American

to take a stand and write to congress and VOTE. If they don't they may very well end up in the same situation John and myself are in. What is worse we must take a stand so our children have hope to not just survive, but to thrive without welfare. Work and new business is the answer not welfare," replies Kitty.

"Your honor the defense rests on the matter of John and Kitty not paying their health insurance," Alice announces to the court.

"With the evidence that has been presented to me today that the defendant not paying their health insurance for seven months; I find the defendant guilty as charged .The fine is twenty thousand dollars or one year in the federal internment camp; the defendant also has to pay two hundred fifty dollars for court costs and their defense attorney fees," says Judge Smith.

"Your honor my clients can not pay the fine they have no choice to go to the federal interment camp," replies Alice.

Uncle Billy gets Alice's attention, and whispers in Alice's ear that John and Kitty's friends will pay the court costs and attorneys fees. Several collections are being circulated to cover the court costs and attorney's fees. Even Alice contributes to help and smiles.

"Your honor I would like to present to the court the donations of John and Kitty's friends to pay the court costs; I also consider my attorney fees paid in full," smiles Alice, announcing to the court.

The bailiff takes the donations to Judge Smith, and even Judge Smith contributes to the collection.

"Mr and Mrs. Kadiddlehopper you certainly have a lot of friends," says Judge Smith. In the gallery everyone is smiling

"You can not take it with you, your honor," replies John. (*Line Lionel Barrymore "You Can Not Take it With You", 1936*)

"We need to find a suitable temporary guardian for the children," says Judge Smith.

"Your honor we petition the court to make Billy Kadiddlehopper temporary guardian of John and Kitty's children," Alice announces to the court.

Alice gives the paperwork to Judge Smith for approval to have Billy Kadiddlehopper temporary guardian to the children.

"I count three DWI's in the last ten years; I do not consider him a suitable guardian; they will have to be put in custody of child protective services and put in a foster home," says Judge Smith..

"Your honor Billy has been clean and sober for two years," replies Alice

" I am concerned about the irresponsible behavior of the eight years before the time he has been clean and sober. I order that child protective services take custody of the children as soon as they find a suitable foster home. Until then they can stay with Billy Kaddlehopper. That is the best I can do under the circumstances and be within the law. I sentence John and Kitty to a undisclosed location, for one year, to the federal internment camp and be transported there immediately; court is adjourned," orders Judge Smith.

Beatrice is in tears and all three children hug their parents; the gallery is in a uproar . John and Kitty are escorted by the police to the paddy wagon that is waiting outside. They first have to get threw the four thousand plus demonstrators waiting outside and the KPOW and RHP reporters. One of the KPOW reporters get John and Kitty's attention.

"What is your reaction of being sentenced today?" asks the KPOW reporter.

"Freedom is dying in America if nothing is done about it," replies John.

"Wake up America. What happen to us can happen to you," replies Kitty.

At that point the demonstrators are blocking the path to the paddy wagon. The police have to stun some demonstrators to get to the paddy wagon. At this point it is like the 400 farmers at the north bridge in Concord, Massachusetts in 1775; that shot at the British that started the American Revolution. The Revolution against socialism in Riverdale, Tennessee HAS begun, and is going to being heard around the world. As soon as the police got John and Kitty in the paddy wagon the demonstrators surrounded the paddy wagon, and are rocking the paddy wagon. The drivers were in fear of their lives. They could not drive without hitting demonstrators. Then all of a sudden a demonstrator smashed their sign on the right side of the windshield and cracked it. The sign says "FREE JOHN AND KITTY!" Then another sign is smashed on the left side of the windshield and cracked it too. It say's "IT NEVER SHOULD HAVE HAPPEN!"

Music "Revolution" Beatles 1968

"Driver can you see out of the windshield?" says Kitty.

"Just slightly, I am suppose to deliver you to Chattanooga," says the driver.

"This crowd doesn't want see you take us away," says John laughing.

The police manage to clear a path and the paddy wagon slowly pulls away form the courthouse. They manage to get underway. Along the way is the like the narrow road to Lexington, Massachusetts, where the British fled to Boston in 1775; there are signs to free John and Kitty are all along the road. Each sign is like the paddy wagon is being shot at.

After a two hour drive. They arrive at the Chattanooga train station waiting for them is the train that will take them to the federal internment camp. It runs from Washington to the internment camp. It is all black and they found a steam articulated locomotive from a train museum to pull the train; it is a shining representation of the industrial revolution. The cars are all black and there are no windows; they are converted baggage cars that they load the passengers like cattle. This train has black flags on the locomotive. People that watch the train at intersections call it **"THE DEATH OF FREEDOM EXPRESS."** It is much like the train that took President

Lincoln from Washington to Illinois. after he was assassinated. This train heading to Chicago then on to Nevada.

"This train is much like a funeral train," says John

"It is a grim reminder what happens when people are silent about their freedom," responds Kitty.

John and Kitty board the train there is practically no light on the train they can barely find their way to their seat. They finally get seated.

"Hold me John this train gives me the creeps," says Kitty

John holds Kitty and kisses her.

"We will be doing this a lot while we are in this situation; we have each other that will help us get threw this," responds John.

The sounds of the wheels on the rails, and the lonely whistle from the steam locomotive; they take the long trip at a slow forty five miles an hour. The train stops to take on water and coal in Chicago. In the background is the clickty clack of the trains wheels and a occasional train whistle at the intersections.

"I wonder why we have a steam engine pulling this train," asks Kitty?

"America has the most coal reserves and the water is still free," replies John.

"Well they could have a nuclear powered train," says Kitty

"They probably wanted to make a market for the coal. Some bureaucrat in Washington thought of it and they managed to get this train as surplus rail cars and a steam engine that worked, that's probably how it happened," says John

"They could have a hybrid powered locomotive," says Kitty.

"Lets face it we get a cast a way train for cast away people that are poor. That is the best way I can put it," says John.

"We are in a train when they were in their peak almost everyone took the train. It is like a time warp back to 1940 to the 1950's," says Kitty.

"This train is much like when the USA gathered all the Japanese and sent them to Wyoming during World War II. We are experiencing the same only we are for not paying our health insurance. That is great distress management dear about the train. We keep thinking that way making the best of things, nothing they do to us will bother us," says John.

They slept a lot with Kitty's head on John's shoulder on their journey to the Federal Internment camp one hundred miles from Micaville, Nevada. "The Death of Freedom Express," crossed the great pains of Iowa, Kansas, and Colorado. It stopped in Denver for water and coal, then it chugged up the continental divide. On the way the majestic peaks tower above the train. With the river on one side cliffs on the other the switch backs are prevalent though the mountains. They also go though tunnels, over bridges, and all most to the desert in Utah. A day later the train finally passed through the town of Micaville, Nevada, on the rail spike that only goes to the Federal internment camp. John and Kitty finally exit the train.

"We are not in Riverdale any more," says John.

"From the green grass of Riverdale to the desolate desert of this place it is quite a contrast," says Kitty.

Chapter Three

The internment camp

John and Kitty are led to a hall that they wait to be seen by a social worker for facility entrance orientation. They find a seats and the hall is very crowded. "This place does not have any windows," says John.

"At least when we turn off the lights dear in bed no light is shining in to keep us awake," replies Kitty.

"That is a positive way to look at it. We could be in this orientation mode for days with this many people," implies John.

"Did you see all the halls connect the three floor buildings?" asks Kitty.

"Yes I did," replies John.

Four hours later they are finally are seen by a social worker and are lead to Ms. Stephen office and are seated.

"Welcome to poverty central. I am to assign you beds and give you a orientation. First the good news both of you are assigned beds together and can sleep together as husband and wife. You are to work 40 hours a week responsibility therapy. The pay is $1.25 a hour As a new resident you have three choices. The first is working in the kitchen we now have 22,630 residents. The second is housekeeping. We have eleven miles of halls and 123 restroom and showers that need to be kept clean. The third is grounds maintenance. That is a variety of jobs that have to be done around the facility. What out of the three do you pick John?" asks Ms. Stephen.

"I pick grounds maintenance," replies John.

"You are to report to Mr Akerson in building 380 at 8 AM here is a map how to get there. "What do you pick Kitty?" asks Ms Stephen.

" I pick working in the kitchen," answers Kitty.

"That's a mountain of dishes to clean," says John.

"There are four dinning halls all have dishes to clean and they need help to clean up. You both eat at dining hall three and eat at 12:30PM. Now I have to assign you a building and beds that are living areas that only have a curtain in between each other. I assign building 209 space 734. Here is a map how to get there. Here is bed rolls, a pillow and a blanket. You also have to sign a accountability roster every morning before 8AM, and there is a bed check at 12 midnight. Failure to sign the accountability roster three times or not seen bed check we consider you have escaped the compound. Penalty for the violation, your time here will be doubled that you are to stay here, if found. There is no water for 150 miles; here are some pictures of residents that have tried to escape. The buzzards have the carcasses picked clean, so they are not recognizable," says Ms Stephen.

"Can we mail letters?" replies John.

"Yes John your first letter is free postage the rest you pay the postage. Here is a writing kit," says Ms. Stephen.

" Thank you this kit will be well used," says John.

"Is there any recreation in this place?" asks Kitty.

"No there is not, you both can sleep together though?" replies Ms Stephen

Kitty gives John a look and John smiles.

"Does that mean anything we want as long as we do not disturb anyone?" says Kitty.

"Yes it does, just make sure your able to report to your RT work," replies Ms Stephen.

"I will have someone take you to your room," says Ms Stephen.

So they are directed to their room by Mr. Burr down the long hall that they seam all the same.

"It will take us a year to figure out to know our way around this place," says John.

"It took me a good six months till I stopped going the wrong way," replies Mr Burr.

"Are you here for not paying your heath insurance too Mr Burr?" asks Kitty.

" No I am not. I am here for telling the president , a inappropriate statement, to his face in a town meeting. I am the great, great, great grand son of Arron Burr that shot Alexander Hamilton," replies Mr. Burr.

"So your here as a political prisoner for exercising your constitutional rights of freedom of speech. That is another well kept secret of the federal government. They are sending US Citizens that are political prisoners to this place," says John.

"More to write about John to Senator Jackson. thank you Mr Burr this place has secrets that need to be told to the rest of America," says Kitty.

"Here we are building 209; there are some things I have to warn you about in this place," says Mr. Burr.

They get to John and Kitty's living area.

"THERE IS A SCORPION ON THE WALL!" screams Kitty.

John flicks with a broom to the scorpion in the floor and crushes it with his foot.

"Scorpions creep in at night and you should check your bedding under your bed every time your go to bed. The only way to kill them is to crush them; insecticide does nothing to them. They can inflict a very painful or fatal for some sting," warns Mr. Burr.

"It's the second hand bricks that this place is built with. There are so many cracks in the wall it is not a wonder that we get what roams in the night in the desert here in our living area," says John.

"THERE IS A TARANCTELLA ON THE BED!" screams Kitty.

"I have the feeling I have to check the living area whenever we are here," John flicks the tarantella, with the broom, on the bed to the floor and crushes it.

" Like the scorpion they have to be crushed: they like dark places including bedding. There bite is very painful." There is one other thing they have problems with here," says Mr Burr.

"Whet is that," asks Kitty.

" They have a real problem here with bats. They get in and fly in the buildings. They no more than a pests and all three eat insects. I will leave you two alone and be careful for what creeps in at night," says Mr Burr.

"Hold me John this place has the environment of ½ on a scale one to ten," says Kitty and kisses John.

"We are not in Riverdale any more, All hell can be around us and it does not matter because your with me. Our love for each other is the oasis in this horrible desert with creepy creatures that creep in the night. We will prevail above this. If this is what socialism offers we have seen a environment that belittle it's residents," says John

"Sounds good John now start writing to Senator Jackson to get us out of this place. I'm going to get some sleep," replies Kitty.

John get out his writing kit the facility gave him and writes to Senator Jackson.

John writes his letter to Jackson and it reads like this:

> Dear Senator Jackson,
>
> Myself and my wife Kitty have been sent to the federal interment camp in the middle of the Nevada desert for not paying our federal health insurance. we are two of the twenty two thousand that live here We own a gas station in Riverdale Tennessee that the taxes for everything for all the government programs got to be too much . It is to the point that we had to lapse our government health insurance to pay the taxes that we had to pay. If we did not have to pay all the taxes we would not be in this horrible place. There are creatures ,from the desert, that creep in at night and we have to work slave labor for $1.25 a hour. There is a resident here for political reasons we really have political prisoners in USA.
>
> Please roll back the taxes that put us in this place and repeal replace the health insurance law so this place does not exist; so people are not fined for not paying their heath insurance Do what you can so families like ours never have be split up like ours ever again. We have three children that were put into a foster home. Please free us from this place so we can put our life together and get things back to normal.
>
> Sincerely,
> John and Kitty Kaddlehopper.

After John gets directions and mails his letter to Senator Jackson; John and Kitty eat dinner and sit on a bench outside building 209; it is now nighttime

" Oh Look John all the stars in the sky there is a bit of romance in this place," says Kitty.

Look a meteor shower we can see so clearly," says John.

"It's like angels are streaking across the sky to help us. I know what we are doing after midnight. The power of love with all hell around us. We have to start working tomorrow our slave RT," says Kitty.

John gives Kitty one very long romantic kiss that takes her breath away.

That night as soon as they where accounted in be checked in bed.

"Make love to me John like you never have before. Make us insulated form this what is around us. We must do this so very quietly so no one hears us. It is like we were younger and your mom and dad, when we were first married, and they are in the next room. Ever so quietly, with all the passion; with the angels in heaven among us," says Kitty

"This night and every night we are here will make our marriage ever so stronger with all the despair here. No matter what makes us dislike this place our love for each other will prevail in this hell around us," replies John.

That night and every night they make love to each other while they in are the internment camp just after bed check..

Chapter Four

Mr Jackson in Washington

The story continues in Senator Jackson's office and he is working on the elections amendment to the constitution elect presidents by the only the popular vote.

"Ms Smitherpoo how are we doing on the elections amendment to be presented to the committee?" says Andrew.

"The amendment should be ready next week for committee. We received this letter from John and Kitty Kaddlehopper they are in the federal internment camp," says Ms Smitherpoo and shows Andrew the letter.

He reads the letter.

"I did not know they sent people to internment camps for not paying their health insurance. We have to put a stop to this and roll back the taxes that put them in this place. Close the interment camp down for good. We must repeal the income tax increases, the federal property tax, the small business tax and the taxes on health insurance companies that caused the insurance companies to pull out of the business. Above all finally repeal and replace the health insurance bill," says Andrew.

"You will have so much resistance Andrew every senator that has a pet program will be against you every step you take," replies Ms Smitherpoo

"I don't care there is twenty two thousand US citizens in the middle of the desert that are suffering so they can have those pet programs. We have families that are being split up that I am sure they did not want that. No we are going to roll back socialism to the point it does not run everyone's life that's what we are to do . We want to get the taxes so the middle class families can make a living without being taxed to being put in a interment camp in the middle of the desert. We will call the bill the Kadiddlehopper Bill. How soon can we get started," says Andrew?

"I can start on it right now ready for committee in two weeks," replies Ms Smitherpoo.

"OK Fine make it so. Ms Smitherpoo what is your first name," asks Andrew?

"Cecile," says Cecile.

" Tomorrow is Independence Day; I'd love for you to accompany me to tour the Washington Monument and see the fireworks at the top?" asks Andrew.

" I accept, it sounds like fun," says Cecile.

Andrew and Cecile walk up to the Washington Monument they walk inside.

"No more Washington's will come in our time," Andrew reads out laud to Cecile.

"There is 199 memorial stones inside, we have to climb the 897 steps to the top to see them," says Cecile.*(The stairway is now closed in 2010)*

" I thought the stairway was closed October 15th 1966," says Andrew.

"They opened it up last year after renovating the stairway," replies Cecile.

"Well lets go up the steps and see all the stones from the states. By the time they start the fireworks display we will be at the top," says Andrew.

" Look Andrew there is the stone from Tennessee," says Cecile.

"There is the one from Arkansas," says Andrew almost out of breath.

"The stones from New Hampshire and Oregon," says Cecile.

They get to the top and at the viewing point kiss each other one very long romantic kiss.

"Oh look Andrew the fireworks," says Cecile!

"They look fantastic and very patriotic. You can see the reflection of the fireworks on the water on the capitol mall," replies Andrew

"This so cool seeing them from up here. I'm glad we came up here to see them. Oh look more fireworks in Arlington and Falls Church, Virginia. The moon is so bright and shimmering on the Potomac, how romantic," says Cecile.

"I have a idea, I'm a member of the Senator Canoe Club; do .you want to go out on the Potomac for a moon light cruse," says Andrew.

"Anything to get out of this heat and humidity. I love how spontaneous you are Andrew. Lets take the elevator down," says Cecile and kisses Andrew.

"We will take my car," says Andrew and they walk to his car.

"How long have you been a member of the Senator Canoe club?" asks Cecile riding in his car.

"As long as I have been a senator; I needed a way to relieve some stress and this weather in the summer on the water is the best way to cool off," says Andrew.

" So I am in good hands in the canoe," says Cecile.

" I know my low brace that helps some," says Andrew

" Well it's so hot and humid tonight; I would not mind a swim if we got wet," replies Cecile.

"I'm the boss in the canoe there is no time for arguments," says Andrew.

"Except when we are to hit a snag," replies Cecile and they walk to the boat house.

"You know that this boat house was built in 1906; we will take out a standard canoe and here is a life jacket," says Andrew.

"Interesting, Do I have to wear a life jacket," says Cecile?

"Yes dear that water still has current; it does not look it has any current. It is night time so I want to be safe," says Andrew and they get in the canoe.

They paddle across the river and startle some ducks.

"Oh the moon shimmering on the river how romantic; this is defiantly worth it. I am still hot and sticky though," says Cecile.

"Yes this is_____NICE," says Andrew and Cecile stands up and jumps in the water the opposite side Andrew is bracing and causes Andrew to fall in the water too.

With a big splash they both are in the water.

" WEEE oh this feels so good!" yells Cecile and she swims to Andrew and kisses him.

"Keep your feet facing downstream Cecile and swim to the shore and hold the canoe, down stream from us," says Andrew.

They pull the canoe up on shore and secure it and walk up on the bank.

"Oh look the moon tonight is so bright," implies Cecile.

"I saw in a movie once to lasso the moon for you. This is 2015 I'll take you to the moon and back instead," says Andrew.

"Mr. Jackson is that a promise? I'll hold you to it," says Cecile.

"To the moon and back," says both of them!

They hug each other and passionately kiss each other. Then the sound
of a airliner interrupts their moment and they look up.

"I have to take you home, staying out in this hot and humid weather it is hard to sleep," says Andrew.

"I agree," replies Cecile.

They both get back in the canoe, ferry across the river, and put the canoe and paddles back in the boat house then lock it up. They walk to Andrew's car and drive to Cecile's place.

In the car they chat.

"I had a fabulous time Andrew the fireworks from the Washington monument will never forget it made me proud to be a American, and most of all I spent it with you," says Cecile.

"I'll walk you to the door. It has been in paradise in heaven for me. Tomorrow do want to visit the Jefferson Memorial? Meet you for lunch then more Independence Day memorial," says Andrew.

"Sounds grand Andrew," replies Cecile.

Andrew kisses Cecile with a kiss that takes her breath away.

"Meet you at eleven in the morning," says Andrew.

"Eleven is fine," says Cecile.

Andrew walks off and looks back.

"To the Moon and Back," yells both of them!

They both wave to each other and Andrew drives off.

The next morning Andrew picks Cecile up and walks to the door and knocks on Cecile's.

She answers the door.

"Are you ready," asks Andrew?

" I sure am been looking forward to it all morning," replies Cecile.

They both drive to the Jefferson Memorial.

"So how soon will the Kadiddlehopper Bill be ready to debate in congress," says Andrew?

"Next week Andrew it gets out of committee. You know it is going to be a up hill battle. Have you told Senator Petabone that your repealing his law. I found out the Earnest Peabody finances his campaign and is the biggest tycoon in all of Tennessee," replies Cecile.

"Tomorrow I present the Amendment to the 12th Amendment to the Constitution to congress for the presidential election to be solely on the popular vote. I have to a chat with Senator Petabone for his support. I will explain why I am repealing his law he wrote. I counted I am repealing 26 other groups appropriation laws. I want to cut taxes by 25% all across the board for every kind of tax you can think of. If Earnest Peabody is in his office he will not like it. What do you want for lunch," asks Andrew?

"A Ruben sandwich, there is a place on the left that has good ones. If you ask me that Ernest Peabody is up to no good. I am pulling all 3000 pages of the health insurance law to see if there is any sneaky appropriations," says Cecile.

"I would not be surprised that there is some pork. I am sure no one read the part about the internment camp in Nevada. I am sure not many read the bill when it came up on to vote," says Andrew.

Andrew parks the car and they both go in Eddy's Restaurant.

"We would like a booth," says Andrew to the waitress.

Both Andrew and Cecile sit at the booth.

"Can I take your order?" asks Claire the waitress.

"Are you Senator Jackson?" asks Claire.

"Yes I am," replies Andrew

"I saw your press conference on TV something about a internment camp in Nevada," says Claire.

"I am presenting the Kadiddlehopper Bill next week to congress to close down the internment camp and repeal 27 groups of appropriation laws, and cut taxes 25%," says Andrew.

"Look out Senator Jackson is going to put the government on the right path. I am sure you will have a lot of resistance," says Claire.

Cecile nods yes.

"We like to order now," says Andrew.

"We would like two Ruben sandwiches with heavy horseradish," says Cecile

"Two Ruben Sandwiches heavy horseradish. You want anything to drink?" say Claire.

" We will have just water, thank you," says Andrew.

Claire leaves the table to deliver their order.

"You know Andrew it may not be that hard to get the Kadiddlehopper bill passed. I know you will have public opinion in your favor in spite the resistance in congress," says Cecile.

"I know there are going to be some senators that will try to stop me. I just have to stick in there and let public opinion prevail," says Andrew.

I had fun yesterday, especially our splash in the river," says Cecile.

"Defiantly spontaneous I wish you told me your jumping out of the canoe so I could brace for it," says Andrew

"Oh quit being a stick in the mud, we both had fun," replies Cecile.

Claire comes to the table with their order then leaves the table.

"Here is your order with two glasses of water. I want to warn you that horseradish is very hot," says Claire.

" I like sandwiches with a kick to them," says Andrew.

Andrew takes one bite and fans his mouth and drinks some water. His eyes wider than normal with his nose full of fumes from the horseradish.

"I like hot and spicy men," giggles Cecile.

"Hot isn't the word for it, more like fuming. Good sandwich though," Says Andrew.

" So you like the paces I pick to eat," replies Cecile.

"I love everything about you Cecile," says Andrew.

"I love everything about you too," says Cecile.

"I hope it is not crowded at the Jefferson Memorial," says Andrew

"It is the fourth of July weekend it is a good possibility that it has quite a few visitors," replies Cecile.

"I am done with my sandwich, it was great if you have a cold," says Andrew

"Yes they are, I will be done in a bit and we will leave," replies Cecile.

They pay the check and leave Eddy's Restaurant and drive to the Jefferson Memorial. At the Jefferson Memorial they walk in where the Decoration Independence is on the wall they see a 8 year old boy reading the declaration of independence out loud. Both Andrew and Cecile listen as he reads what is on the wall.

"We hold these truths to be self-evident that all men are created equal, that they are endowed by their Creator with certain inalienable rights, among these are life, liberty, and the pursuit of happiness, that to secure these rights governments are instituted among men. We...solemnly publish and declare, that these colonies are and of right ought to be free and independent states...And for the support of this declaration, with a firm reliance on the protection of divine providence, we mutually pledge our lives, our fortunes, and our sacred honor," says Stephen Shambach.

Andrew gets Stephen's attention and is on one knee.

"What is your name?" says Andrew.

"My name is Stephen Shambach," he shakes Andrew's hand as he says it.

"Stephen my name is Senator Jackson. Where you learn to read like that, Stephen?" asks Andrew.

"My third grade teacher and my father by reading to me then I learned to read my own stories. This is my father that taught me," answers Stephen.

"I am pleased to meet you Mr. Shambach your son is impressive reading the Declaration of Independence," says Andrew.

"I am honored to meet you Senator Jackson," says Mr Shambach.

"I am debating congress tomorrow on abolishing the electoral college. I would like to quote Stephen's reading ability to show how far our country has come concerning the literacy level in 2015," says Andrew

"Senator you have my full support. That is something that is long overdue to change that how presidents are elected," says Mr Shambach.

"Thank you Mr Shambach for your support," says Andrew

On the other wall Cecile is witnessing 9 year old Joan reading out loud about the separation of church and state.

"Almighty God hath created the mind free...All attempts to influence it by temporal punishments or burthens...are a departure from the plan of the Holy Author of our religion...No man shall be compelled to frequent or support any religious worship or ministry or shall otherwise suffer on account of his religious opinions or belief, but all men shall be free to profess and by argument to maintain, their opinions in matters of religion. I know but one code of morality for men whether acting singly or collectively," says Joan Jenson.

"That was very good reading. What is your name. I'm Cecile," says Cecile?

Senator Jackson joins them.

" I am Joan Jenson, I know who you are you're Senator Jackson," says Joan.

Senator Jackson shakes Joan's hand.

"I saw you on the Internet are you going to free John and Kitty" asks Joan?

"Next week I address congress for the debate to free them and 22000 plus Americans that are there too," answers Andrew.

" I do not want to grow up and face that problem. Please promise me you will make sure that internment camp is demolished to the ground," says Joan.

"I sure will and everything connected to it" replies Andrew

"Joan, you see that what is on the roof," says Andrew

" You mean, I have sworn upon the altar of God eternal hostility against every form of tyranny over the mind of man," says Joan.

"Next week I fight to make sure this country stays free from tyranny that threatens our freedom. Tomorrow I am working on abolishing the electoral congress," says Andrew.

"Bye Senator Jackson remember your promise to me," says Joan

"I will Joan, I promise," replies Andrew.

Andrew and Cecile's relationship starts with the night sky lighting up!

Stephen and Joan the future of United States of America

Chapter Five

Senator Jackson on the Senate Floor, amending the
Twelfth Amendment To the Constitution.

The Vice President is taking role attendance and giving the results in the senate chamber.

"The Role 99 present and one absent, there is a quorum. Are there any bills to be presented to the floor," says Vice President Quinn?

"Mr. President I am presenting a bill, SB361, to amend the twelfth amendment of constitution to abolish the electoral college. Elect presidents only by the popular vote," says Senator Jackson.

"The chair recognizes Senator Jackson, proceed with your debate Senator Jackson," says Vice President Quinn.

"Gentlemen let me remind you of the election of 1824 my Great, great grandfather General Andrew Jackson had the highest percentage of 41% of the four that were running for president with the popular vote. He did not receive enough electoral votes having the most out of the four candidates. The election was brought to the house of representatives with clever political maneuvering in he house of representatives elected John Quincy Adams became our 6th president. In spite of not having as much popular vote as Andrew Jackson did.

When Andrew Jackson was finally elected president he was a strong avocet to amend the 12th amendment of the constitution every year he was president, like I am today. If you lost a election like the one in 1824 it is no wonder you would try to correct it. If the election was based on the popular vote Andrew Jackson would have won the election of 1824.

The electoral college was enacted partially because of the literacy rate of the United States is not as high now in 2015. They had to be property owners too. Yesterday I visited the Jefferson Memorial and I witnessed 8 year old Stephen Shambach recited on the wall Decoration of Independence. Today gentlemen that is enough evidence to me that there is maybe only .5% or less of the US citizens that does not know how to read. Today's United States citizens can make intelligent decisions picking a candidate for president s by them selves without the electoral college. If we have a election like 1824 with three or four candidates we can have a winner that won with the highest percentage of the popular vote.

In 1970 and 1971 in the senate attempt, amending the 12th amendment was not successful and nothing has been done till now. The reason in 1971 the failure of passage the small states would be not as significant as the states with more population. If a candidate gets heavy vote in several small population states they still can win elections. In fact a third party candidate has a better chance of winning with the popular vote than with the electoral college. With the popular vote it does not matter what state the votes come from.

I ask Mr Preasadant to put SB361 to vote after it is seconded," says Andrew.

"I second it, I agree with Senator Jackson the people do no longer need a electoral college to vote for them. They are smart enough to make their own decisions. This will work if we make sure who votes are citizens of the USA when they vote. We have been electing senators and congressmen by the popular vote for years," says Senator Petabone of Tennessee.

"SB361 is up for a vote all senators are summoned to vote for this bill it needs 60 votes to pass," says Vice President Quinn

The pages scurry for the senators not on the floor to vote for SB361, and vote is taken.

"SB361 passes 63 for 36 Nay votes the 12th Amendment to the constitution. SB361 has to be ratified by the states to amend the constitution to abolish the electoral college," announced by Vice President Quinn.

After the session Andrew gets Senator Petabone's attention in the hall.

"Senator Petabone I would like to thank you for your support to SB361," says Andrew.

"It should have been done a long time ago no matter what party they are affiliated with. We accomplished the easy part done now to get ratification from the states," says Senator Petabone.

"I have a matter to discuss with you about the health insurance bill. Next week I am submitting a bill to repeal and replace the health insurance law," says Andrew.

"I like to discuss this in my office. Would 1 PM Monday be OK?" asks Senator Petabone.

"Monday at 1 PM is fine," replies Andrew.

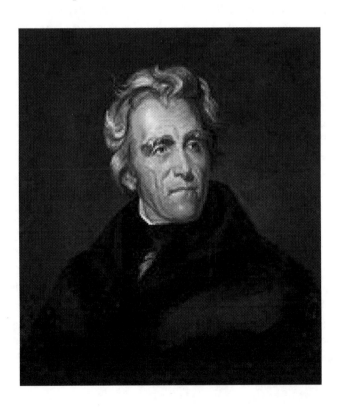

Chapter Six

The Politics off the Senate Floor, Andrew's and Cecile's Sexology

Senator Jackson is in Senator Petabone's office for the appointment they made on Friday.

"I like to see Senator Petabone," says Andrew to Senator Petabone's legal secretary.

"He is expecting you; go a head and go right in," says Senator Petabone's legal Secretary. Senator Jackson goes in Senator Petabone's office

"Good Afternoon John (Petabone) I have run into a predicament I have to repeal your health insurance legislation. Did you know when they passed the law they have internment camps in the middle of Nevada? I have some of my constituents that are being held there for not paying their health insurance," says Andrew

"I herd they made some amendments to the health insurance law. I did not hear what they were. We can have the law amended to close down the internment camp," says Senator Petabone.

"I want to repeal it is a bad law it has no provisions to have the insurance companies be the actuary and no comprehensive tort reform. No encouragement for completion across state lines, no provisions to hold down costs like a hospital charging $10 for tissue paper. Families being broken up because the parents fall behind on their bills. No I will fight you on this. Says Andrew.

"I will support you closing down the internment camp not to repeal the health insurance law," says Senator Petabone

"I am also repealing 26 other entitlement laws and cutting taxes 25% to get the country working again. The country in two months will be bankrupt nether you or I will have a job as we know it now unless the government gets it's house in order. We have to make some serious cut backs and shut down this idea of a free lunch for everyone and socialism. We have to get people working again on real jobs that pay their fair share of taxes. I don't want citizens not being able to pay there bills because they have to pay too much in taxes," says Andrew.

"I have certain powerful commitments concerning the health insurance law that I can not disclose to you Andrew. Please do not pursue this course of action repealing the health insurance law," says Senator Petabone.

"Come when the Kadiddlehopper bill comes up for debate I will be on the floor with or without your support," Says Andrew.

"Andrew please don't fight me on this. I am for getting those people out of the internment camp isn't that enough," says Senator Petabone

"No sir it is not enough! It sounds like Thursday I will have my share of resistance without your support, Good bye Senator, I will see you on the senate floor," replies Andrew.

Andrew storms out of senator Petabone's office.

Senator Petabone calls Earnest Peabody on the phone. Earnest Peabody is the richest tycoon in Tennessee and funds Senator Petabone's campaign

"Earnest we have a problem your government appropriation for your malls is in jeopardy. Senator Jackson Thursday is submitting a bill to repeal the health insurance law. Your appropriation for your malls will be stopped if his bill passes. Can you come to Washington?" asks Senator Petabone.

"Yes that issue is important to me. Things here will have to wait. I will be on the on my plane for Washington," replies Earnest Peabody.

Earnest Peabody is well dressed in a three piece suit with a very pretty personal secretary that goes everywhere he goes, her name is Stephanie. Earnest Peabody takes this plane to Washington and meets Senator Petabone in his office the next morning.

"What reason is Senator Jackson reason to want to repeal the health insurance bill," asks Earnest Peabody?

"There is a provision in the health insurance law that allows an internment camp in the middle of Nevada and I agree with him to shut down the interment camp. He wants repeal the law entirely and replace it with a law that is not out of budget, and put provisions in it that is not in the present law," Replies senator Petabone.

"I employ 120 employees in my mall I would have to pay their salaries myself," says Earnest Peabody.

"The problem is I made the appropriation for one person. The Ethics Committee will fry me alive if they find out about the appropriation I made to you. It be hard to explain why tax payer money is used for a private enterprise that is not authorized," says Senator Petabone.

"Let me talk to Senator Jackson maybe we can convince him to take another course of action to close down the internment camp," says Earnest Peabody.

"I will call Andrew and make a appointment to be in my office tomorrow. Hello Andrew can you be my office tomorrow? Is noon for lunch OK?" asks Senator Petabone on the phone.

" Yes that is fine. I will see you at Noon for lunch," says Andrew on the phone.

"Fine we will all have a talk with Senator Jackson tomorrow. Stephanie let's go to a nice place to eat. We are out on the town," says Earnest Peabody.

Before the meeting the next day Earnest Peabody has a chat with Stephanie.

"Stephanie I want you to be especially, "nice," to Senator Jackson. He will be here for lunch," says Earnest Peabody.

"Sure Boss," says Stephanie.

Senator Jackson enters the room.

"Thanks for coming on such short notice Andrew. I like you to meet Earnest Peabody and this is secretary Stephanie. Won't you have a seat," says John (Petabone).

Andrew shakes both Earnest Peabody's hand Stephanie's hand. Stephanie is very flirtatious toward Andrew.

"Nice to meet you," Says Andrew and sits down.

Stephanie sits in Andrews lap with her arms around Andrew and caressing Andrew.

"Hi Baby your cute," says Stephanie.

"You can forgive Stephanie's friendly nature," says Earnest Peabody.

"That's quite all right I sort of like the attention. Just what did you want to talk to me about," says Andrew and smiles at Stephanie.

"I understand you have a internment camp in Nevada that you want to close down. I could not agree more that needs to be done. You want to repeal the health insurance law," says Earnest Peabody.

"The law needs to be repealed and replaced I am doing just that Thursday," replies Andrew.

"I could make financing your next election for Senator very easy if you just make it a amendment to the old one. A support for running for President," says Earnest Peabody.

"No Sir your lobbying me does not do you any good I want to see John privately. Stephanie please get off my lap," says Andrew and meets John in the next room.

"What do you want to discuss with me," says senator Petabone

"What is in the health insurance law that concerns Earnest Peabody and how much has he contributed to your election campaign," asks Andrew?

"Andrew do you think I would draft legislation for one person it would be totally unethical if I did that. Earnest Peabody has contributed considerable to my campaign fund within federal election law guidelines," replies John(Petabone).

"Cecile is combing the health insurance law and if I find that you have made appropriation to one citizen of Tennessee, namely Earnest Peabody. I will have you before the Ethics Committee. Your in Earnest Peabody's side pocket, and .your only a mere puppet for him. You can have all the graft and corruption. I will not stand for it, Good Bye John I will see you on the Senate Floor," says Andrew.

On the way out of the office Andrew sees Earnest Peabody.

"Mr Peabody you can keep all your money and graft and corruption. It is people like you that gives Washington a bad name. Stephanie you deserve better than to hang around with that man. Money is not everything in life!" says Andrew.

"Sure Baby!" replies Stephanie.

Senator Petabone meets with Earnest Peabody.

"John he is going to be a problem, I can take care of it," says Earnest Peabody.

"Senator Jackson is being a very good senator I do not want you to do anything to discredit him. I knew his father and he was just as ethical as he is. His father was known for fighting lost causes. I just hope that Andrew is not fighting a lost cause too," says Senator Petabone.

"Just say the word and I will have public opinion changed against him," says Earnest Peabody.

Andrew gets back to his office and Cecile is there working.

"Cecile how soon will you have the proof that Earnest Peabody is receiving a appropriation from the Health Insurance Law," says Andrew.

"I am on page 1998 I will have the proof very soon," replies Cecile.

"Earnest Peabody just tried to lobby me and his secretary, Stephanie, flirted with me and said I am cute," says Andrew.

" I agree, you are cute dear. The Kadiddlehopper Bill I have ready for you to debate in the Senate for Thursday," says Cecile.

"So what else did this Stephanie do to you," asks Cecile?

"She sat on my lap. I am hungry, let go to that sandwich place Eddies,"
says Andrew.

"Did she get your attention," asks Cecile?

"She acted like a common whore to be honest. I did not even know her. Lets go out to eat," replies Andrew.

They leave the office to eat lunch. They drive to the restaurant, and
they talk in the car driving, on the way to the restaurant

"Did you react any sexually with her sitting on your lap," asks Cecile?

"Yes unwillingly, the oxytocin was flowing," says Andrew, red faced.

"I think if you two were alone and you did not have to stand up for your principles you would have gone farther. I think your a very sexy, spontaneous and spicy guy Andrew," says Cecile.

William Quayle Jr.

"Well I did not so there is not anything to discuss about Stephanie," says Andrew.

"Sooner or later, as two intelligent heterosexuals, we have to chat about our sexology Andrew," says Cecile.

"Let's not go there and talk dirty Cecile," says Andrew.

"There is a difference in being academic sexually than just plain dirty sex there is a big difference. Like do you want any children?" asks Cecile

They arrive to the restaurant and Claire is there greet them and to sit them at the table.

"HI Claire we like a booth," says Andrew.

They both is at the booth

I'd like a Ruben sandwich heavy on the horseradish and water to drink," says Andrew to Claire.

"I will have the same," says Cecile.

"Yes I want children, be married and have a little boy like Steven that was at the Jefferson Memorial. I am into a long term relationship. No more one night stands.

I am into procreation and responsibility. I do not need contraception wanting children. I do not have any sexual transmitted infections that I know of. If there is a child I don't know about I would take care of it as my own, if I found out about it" says Andrew.

"I want children and be married. Have a little girl like Joan at the Jefferson Memorial. I too want a long term relationship. I do not have any sexual transmitted diseases ether. Do you know about Tantra Andrew," implies Cecile?

"I have your order," says Claire and gives them their order. Andrew eats some of his sandwich.

"This is a good sandwich. No I don't know about Tantra," says Andrew.

Cecile takes a bite of her sandwich and gasps, the fumes come out of her nose, and drinks some water.

" Well Tantra is a ancient practice of practicing sex. We can do some here and still be decent. Stare in my left eye Andrew," says Cecile.

They look into each others left eye for about Five minutes it's like looking into one's soul.

"That's really some thing," says Andrew.

"Eat your sandwich and take me home," says Cecile.

They finish their sandwich and drive to Cecile's place.

"Andrew do you want come in with me," asks Cecile?

"Sure I do not have anything else going," replies Andrew.

Andrew and Cecile went into her place and from there they got to know each other better. What do you think what happen next?

Chapter Seven

Andrew Starts the debate for the
Kaddidehopper Bill and scandal.

"Role call for today Thursday July 14 100 senators present none are absent. Looking on the calendar Senator Jackson has the Kadiddlehopper Bill to be presented for debate," says Vice President Quinn.

"Gentlemen the bill I am presenting is to repeal twenty seven groups of appropriation laws and to cut taxes 25% to keep the government from closing down in two months.

I have a report from the US Treasury Department and the Federal Reserve. It confirms that our credit to keep the government running will no longer be available and the country is officially bankrupt in two months. This means gentlemen that we can no longer to continue social programs. One of these is the health insurance law and hidden in the legislation we do have internment camps in Nevada. I know John and Kitty Kadiddlehopper that they are being held in the internment camp, that are two of the 22000 plus Americans that are being held there. John and Kitty's family has been broken up by the government. We must have the internment camp in Nevada shut down and evacuated. I have arranged the land be turned over to the Air Force and everything that is connected to the area be destroyed. The area is to be used as a new target area for a new secret weapon, the B2015," says Andrew.

"Will Senator Jackson yield!" yells Senator Petabone.

"Yes I will yield," answers Senator Jackson.

"Just today I have received information that Senator Andrew Jackson V is unfit to be a member of this body and present any kind of legislation. I have found that Senator Jackson is suspect of ethics violation," says Senator Petabone assertively.

There is a uproar on the senate floor and in the gallery.

"Order, Order," says Vice President Quinn.

"Mr President I motion that I have a continuance till I can clear up this accusation of the ethics violation," implies Senator Jackson.

"Motion granted we will have a continuance next Thursday at 12 noon. Please notify me if you have to reschedule Senator Jackson," says Vice President Quinn.

"Thank you Mr President I will," says Senator Jackson.

Cecile and Edward the reporter are in the gallery.

"I smell A RAT!" says Cecile!

"Who is the rat Cecile? I have to be at Senator Jackson's exit this is a hot story about the ethic's scandal," says Edward.

"The rat is Earnest Peabody!" says Cecile.

"Who is Earnest Peabody; You want to go out for dinner?" asks Edward.

"I can't say right now. No I do not want to go out to dinner with you Edward," says Cecile.

Cecile and Edward exit the gallery and meet Andrew exiting the Senate floor.

The press has the exit blocked. Senator Jackson is interviewed with the press.

"Senator is this investigation for ethic's violation any way related to the Kaddidehopper Bill?" asks Edward.

"There is a good possibility it is. Passage of the Kadiddlehopper is essential if the United States is going to exist as a nation. I have a report that the Treasury Department can not issue any more bonds in two months. There is a interment camp where people are being secretly sent there for not paying health insurance. The Kaddidehopper Bill is named after John and Kitty Kadiddlehopper. There is 22,000 plus Americans being held out in the middle of the desert in Nevada," implies Senator Jackson.

"Do you know what the ethic's violation is about," asks a ROX News Reporter?

"No I do not at this time. It is someone that does not want the Kadiddlehopper Bill to be passed. I will know more in tomorrow's investigation," replies Senator Jackson.

The next morning Andrew is before the ethics committee the room is packed with reporters, clerical personnel and senators. Cecile' Stephanie, and Senator Petabone are there. The chairman of the Ethics committee is the Senate minority leader is Senator William Cranberry of Oregon that is presiding.

"The meeting for the Ethic's committee is now in session. On the calendar there is a investigation for inappropriate behavior in June 2008 with a female, Miss Boom, Boom Myrna of Nashville, Tennessee. with Senator Andrew Jackson in his first term of office. How do you plea Senator Jackson?" says Senator Cranberry.

"Not Guilty, what is the details of the complaint?" It happen one month over seven years ago that is pushing past the statue of limitations," replies Senator Jackson.

"It says that you fathered a child named Paul Jackson that is seven years old," replies Senator Cranberry.

"Senator Cranberry that is news to me. I would not willfully be irresponsible to the support of my son. Some times women do not come forward that they are expecting your child. I can not deny having sexual relations with Myrna. I have not been told I am a father. Today is the first time I have been told I am a father. I am willing to take Paul as my own ether adopt or file for custody to be a responsible parent of Paul.

Just the other day at the Jefferson Memorial I wish I would have a son like Stephen Shambach that I saw there reading the declaration of independence. So now you tell me the great news I am a father," says senator Jackson.

"Is this is the first time you have been told about Paul?" (*to be sure*) asks Senator Cranberry.

"Yes sir it is," replies Senator Jackson.

"I do not see any ethics violation Senator Jackson can not be held responsible for the time he did not know about that he is the father of Paul Jackson. It is impressing Senator Jackson you are going to take steps to be responsible for support of your son.

It has been over 7 years that is past the statue of limitations. I find you not guilty. (he smiles) Congratulations Senator Jackson. I want to see senator Petabone in my office after the hearing," says Senator Cranberry.

Andrew and Cecile exit the Ethic's Committee meeting and the ROX News Reporter is waiting outside the room.

"Congratulations Senator Jackson with the news your a father! What is your opinion what went on in the meeting?" asks the ROX news reporter.

"Today it was a lame attempt to stop the Kaddidehopper bill to become law. Today is great news that the family always prevails in good times and in bad. When I take the senate floor again I will not give it up until the Kaddidehopper Bill passes the senate. I don't care how long it takes it is for the existence of the USA. We are at the cross road of certain bankruptcy in two short months or common sense government that runs within it's budget," replies Senator Jackson.

That night Andrew went to the Andrew Jackson Monument in Lafayette Park.

Talking to himself as a daily journal in a way to his great, great grandfather.

"Grandpa we passed the amendment to the 12th Amendment of the constitution for the popular vote. I found out I am a father today. There was in a lame attempt to stop a bill that would make your problem with the United States Bank seam like a party," says Andrew.

Cecile finds Andrew at the monument. *Music the Battle of New Orleans, by Jimmy Horton would be most appropriate.*

"There you are, you ready getting ready for the Battle of New Orleans 2015? You know you have one thing in common with your great, grandfather. If you pass the Kadiddlehopper Bill you have both saved America from certain destruction. Your grandfather from the British. Your saving America from socialism and certain bankruptcy," implies Cecile.

"It is not going to be easy I am not giving up the senate floor for anyone. Did you get the proof about Earnest Peabody getting a appropriation," says Andrew?

"Yes I is that is why I am looking for you. I found it on page 2555. You can use it to really put Senator Petabone in place if you need to use it," says Cecile.

"I am sure Senator Petabone is not the only senator that will give me resistance," says Andrew and kisses Cecile passionately.

Chapter Eight

*Senator Jackson presents the Kadiddlehopper Bill
the second time, the historical Filibuster, and more scandal.*

"The Senate is now in session I would like the tally of the senators present," says Vice President Quinn.

One of the pages delivers the tally.

"We have a quorum there is 99 senators present one absent. The first bill on the Calendar for debate is Senator Jackson's Kadiddlehopper Bill," says Vice President Quinn"

"I object Senator Jackson has not been officially cleared to present any bills to this body!" assertively says Senator Petabone.

"We must wait till the Ethic's Committee's decision is official," says Senator Trent the majority leader.

"Mr President I ruled that there is no Ethic's violation in our last meeting the paperwork has not finished processing. Senator Jackson has not done anything to jeopardize the reputation of the United States Senate," says Senator Cranberry.

"The chair recognizes *with hesitation and smiles* **Senator Jackson,** You may proceed!" says Vice President Quinn.

"Will Senator Jackson yield for a question," asks Senator Petabone.

"No I will not yield for a question. In fact I better do this now; and expose Senator Petabone and the lobbyist tycoon, Earnest Peabody, for gross ethic's violation for making a appropriation to fund a mall in Nashville, Tennessee. The appropriation specifically says that Earnest Peabody gets five million dollars a year   This is tax payer money an illegal appropriation that is in the Health Insurance law that was passed in 2010. The illegal appropriation was well hid in the law on page 2555. This is the reason Senator Petabone tried to peg a ethics violation on me to stop me from repealing the health insurance law

I formally now request that Senator John Petabone is impeached by the US Senate immediately," says senator Jackson.

"May I see the health insurance law," asks Vice President Quinn?

A page takes the law to Vice President Quinn and gives it to him. There is two minutes of silence"

"Senator Petabone I have not seen such misrepresentation since I have been in politics. I will be swift in this case so Senator Jackson can present the Kadiddlehopper bill to this body. I am asking for a vote that Senator John Petabone is impeached for a gross ethics violation. I am doing this on the basis what is written in the health insurance law, and there is no hearing with the Ethic's Committee. It be just a needless delay of justice to delay the senates action. There needs to be seventy six votes for impeachment of Senator John Petabone," says Vice President Quinn.

There is a uproar in the gallery and on the senate floor, the vote is taken to impeach Senator Petabone.

"Senator Petabone is getting caught with his hand in the cookie jar too often," says Cecile to Edward the reporter.

"What a story, Vice President Quinn takes swift action to impeach Senator Petabone," says Edward the Reporter.

" The voting results to impeach Senator John Petabone for ethics violation and misrepresentation, Eighty one for impeachment, eighteen against. Mr. Petabone you hereby asked to leave the senate floor. .You will be fined as well for $50000 and forfeiture of retirement pay," says Vice President Quinn.

"NOOO this can't be. Damn that EARNEST PEABODY and his graft and corruption!" Yells Mr Petabone in a shear nervous breakdown and leaves the floor of the senate.

"Way to go Andrew , Mr. Petabone is being kicked out of the Senate!" cheers Cecile and whistles, gives Andrew thumbs UP.

"History has been made Mr John Petabone was impeached and leaves in disgrace and a nervous wreck. Nothing in the history of the United States has ever been done till now. We have not even got to the main event yet," says Edward the reporter.

"Ex senator Petabone was impeached today and the FBI and the CIA are looking for Earnest Peabody. Senator Jackson exposed the misappropriation on the senate floor today. It is obvious Senator Jackson works for us, and is out to clean house. In this case it is the senate," says ROX news on TV.

Earnest Peabody sees the news cast and is in panic to leave the USA.

"Quick Stephanie we have to pack now and head for my plane. The FBI will be here any minute," says Earnest Peabody in panic to Stephanie.

"Right Baby!" replies Stephanie.

Back on the senate floor Vice President Quinn resumes the senate session.

"Senator Jackson you may proceed presenting your bill to the floor," says Vice President Quinn.

"Gentlemen I am presenting the capitalist counter revolution. We have come the point that there is not enough taxpayers to pay for the social programs that are appropriation benefits that we call socialism.

In 1960 when President John F. Kennedy took office said "Ask Not what the Government can do for you; ask what you can do for your country." *(JFK 1960)* The average middle class family can not make ends meet because of all the taxes they have to pay. I know John and Kitty Kadiddlehopper that own one of the two gas stations in the town of Riverdale, Tennessee. They have been arrested by the IRS for not paying their government health insurance and are now in a internment camp in the middle of Nevada. Their children are with court ordered into foster care because the government did not see the possibility that a perfectly good family is broken up by such lack of foresight. They could pay the health insurance if they were not taxed so heavily that all the rest of the bills they have.

They fell behind and there house is foreclosed their business that the are paying taxes with was closed down too.

The government has come to a cross road ether cut back and reduce taxes and encourage Americans to work and paying taxes OR in two short months the country ceases to exist at all.

Today I am presenting a bill to repeal 27 appropriation laws or groups of appropriations, with the exemption of the food stamp program, for education grants, and Stamford loans. I am also cutting taxes 25% on income and business taxes as well cutting taxes every tax that has been enacted. We must balance the budget NOW and there is not any later. Later is here and now.

"Will the senator yield for a question," Says senator Smith from Kansas.

"I have a long speech please make it short senator Smith," replies Senator Jackson.

"Will this bill repeal my appropriation for a study to save the ring tailed duck," asks Senator Smith.

"Yes it does, it is not absolutely necessary for running the country it is in my bill to repeal unnecessary appropriations. Gentlemen the days of the government giving out money for every little cause is to stop now with this bill," replies Senator Jackson.

"Will Senator Jackson yield for a Question?" asks Senator Burray from California.

"Yes please make it short," replies senator Jackson

"Will the bill affect any military appropriations?" asks Senator Burray.

 "No it will not, it is not a social program," answers Senator Jackson.

"I am also reforming heath care so it is not as expensive and does not cost any more if we did not have it. What is badly needed is comprehensive tort reform to put the accident injury attorneys virtually out of business and practice a different practice of law. Malpractice insurance pays a set amount without arbitration. Enact a medial code system to pay a set amounts for certain claims. This will eliminate the need to go to court in most cases. The bottom line the doctors and hospitals pay lower premiums for their malpractice insurance and they still have to be responsible for giving service. A claim can not receive any more than what is set in the schedule for payment for a malpractice claim.

This is long over due, the federal government offer national insurance licenses that have higher fiscal requirements than the state requirements. This will allow insurance companies to sell across state lines for all types of insurance not just health insurance. The commerce department will issue the licenses and the department will receive fees enough to budget the added service to the insurance companies. For the insurance companies it will save time and money and they do not have to be licensed in 50 individual states like they do now.

Keeping a lid on hospital bills is what this bill does best. If we keep costs low the insurance rates will go down.

Mr President I am asking something unusual. I would like to ask for a vote and not give up the floor if this bill does not pass," says Senator Jackson.

"Under the circumstances permission granted we will have a vote of the Kaddidehopper Bill we need 60 votes for passage. The bill is not dead if it does not pass," says Vice President Quinn.

The pages scurry to announce the vote and the vote is taken.

There is silence then Vice President Quinn announces the vote 58 for and 41 against the bill fails to pass. Senator Jackson you have the floor," says Vice President Quinn.

"It looks like we are going to be here for a long time. I will filibuster as long as it takes until the Kadiddlehopper Bill passes," implies Senator Jackson.

"This is news Senator Jackson filibusters the senate," say Edward the reporter to Cecile in gallery.

"We have discussed this problem getting the bill passed ; I will work on getting faxes, email and the notify social web sites to get public opinion," says Cecile to Edward.

"ROX News, Senator Jackson is now filibustering the senate to pass the Kadiddlehopper Bill to free John and Kitty and the 22000 plus residents for not paying their health insurance. It is do or die situation to save the United States of America of certain bankruptcy"

The Coffee Party saw the news cast and organized a demonstration in front of the capitol building they have a standing permit to demonstrate and to support Senator Jackson the next morning.

If I am to play a song it would be," God save the USA", Lee Greenwood.

Demonstrators are chanting Free John and Kitty, Pass the Bill, Train wreck the Death of Freedom Express. By mid afternoon 500,000 plus demonstrators are chanting so loud when they open the senate doors they can hear them.

The police close down the demonstration almost triggering a riot.

In the mean time Senator Jackson's stamina is showing he has been addressing congress for 20 hours and still going strong with his big voice.

The next morning the news got around that Senator Jackson needed help from the public. The demonstrator numbers are now double what they were the day before and exceed one million. Senator Jackson's office is inundated with faxes ,email and every other kind of communication that is prevalent in 2015.

"ROX news: Senator Jackson has been filibustering for over 20 hours, this is democracy in it's finest in a most noble cause, Senator Jackson is our champion of freedom to save the country of certain bankruptcy. To slash and dash, to kill socialism and get America working again," announces the ROX news Reporter

Outside the senate, the senators are wondering when Senator Jackson is going to let up he has now held the senate floor for 23 hours.

"I support him what he is doing something we should have done a long time ago. He is honest and has integrity something that is needed in the senate. We have to reverse the spending spree and no cuts in the budget," says Senator Cranberry.

"I really like him as a senator, I have not seen anyone like him in 20 years," says Vice President Quinn

"He is right that the country is going to be bankrupt if nothing is done to stop the deficit spending and roll back socialism," says Senator Smith.

The senators and Vice President Quinn. enter the senate and Senator Jackson is still addressing the senate "Role call 98 senators present two absent there is a quorum, Senator Jackson still holds the floor," says Vice President Quinn

"Good morning lady's and gentlemen it is great day to pass a bill.

One of the reasons my great grandfather closed down the United States Bank is the use of credit for the fiscal basis of the economy. Our paper money is only a loan on the federal reserve that is backed up by worthless treasury notes. In a sense the money supply is based on loans and not real value on our money. When Andrew Jackson was president the national debt was a mere $34,000. Now we are over 20 trillion dollars for our national debt.

We must make our money no longer a worthless loans; we must make our money worth something. The best way to make our money worth something is use silver and gold.

I avocet we have to get away from worthless federal notes. Then we can rapidly repay our national debt. We can show the world that we are getting our fiscal house in order. When you get a United States Dollar that is silver we make our currency sound our country becomes stronger. This Bill discontinues the federal reserve note; when you have a silver coin then our money is real. It will cause the silver mines (*of Nevada)* of our country to boom like they have done in the past. The bankers will not like it because of handling the weight of the silver . When our money increase, with silver, in value we will be able to buy more than with inflation it is less. The government must now work on a budget it can no longer afford to just print money to stay on the national budget. WE have come to the point we can no longer issue bonds to the federal Reserve to print more money.

If we don't make this change the United States will cease to exist as a country. The currency of our country when it is strong our economy is strong too."

Senator Jackson walks to the senate door and open it. They can hear the demonstrators outside chanting free John and Kitty and train wreck the Death of freedom express.

"Pages I want you to bring all the faxes that have I received just over night from my office," says Senator Jackson.

The pages bring in 500,000 plus faxes from Senator Jackson's office

"The faxes are from every state in the union. I read a fax from Abby Clement from White Plains, New York.

Don't give up Senator Jackson, What your doing to roll back socialism is worth fighting for. God Save the USA.

Signed
Abby Clement

These faxes and emails are from all over the country your constituents. Ladies and gentlemen listen to the people OUR BOSS.

Patrick Henry said, "give me liberty or give me death," slowly saying the last line," says Senator Jackson Andrew faints in shear exhaustion to the floor. Senator Jackson is completely out of it.

"Andrew!" yells Cecile from the gallery and the senate floor is not quiet

"Mr President I ask for Senator Jackson for a vote of the bill!" yells senator Cranberry.

"Pages notify senators for a vote," says Vice President Quinn

The Vote is taken the and paramedics carry Senator Jackson off the floor.

"The Kaddidehopper Bill passes 97 yes one abstain vote, well he just was carried out," says Vice President Quinn smiling.

Cecile goes to Andrew's side he comes to while he is on the gurney she kisses him.

"You did it darling the vote was unanimous. I am so proud of you. Senator Cranberry asked for a vote for you," says Cecile.

"I did, I have to thank senator Cranberry where is he?" asks Andrew.

Cecile gets senator Cranberry and he is beside Senator Jackson.

"You get some rest OLE Hickory (Senator Jackson) you have a son to see," says Senator Cranberry smiling

"Thanks for asking for the vote, So I have," says Senator Jackson.

On TV ROX News.

"Senator Andrew OLE Hickory Jackson V today rolls back taxes and the health insurance law is repealed and replaced and 26 other groups of appropriations is repealed. The internment camp in Nevada that houses 22000 plus residents is now to be closed down , evacuated and destroyed by the Air Force. The Federal reserve note is now history our money is to be exchanged for silver or gold," says ROX reporter

Chapter Nine

Closure of the internment camp,
Senator Jackson puts John and Kitty's lives back together.

It was not until October 1 2015 they finally started to evacuate the Federal interment camp in Nevada. The Death of Freedom Express is decorated red white and blue. The trains cars were changed to regular passenger cars with windows that had the same declarations. The train was transformed from the train of doom to the train of liberty. After all they could not just let 22000 people be stranded in the desert. They had to have a way to get them home.

Andrew and Cecile was not going to wait till John and Kitty's turn to take the train, and chartered a helicopter to pick John and Kitty up. Andrew searches for Ms Stephan to be led to building 209 were John and Kitty are staying.

" I am looking for John and Kitty Kaddidehopper can you take me to evacuate them?" says Senator Jackson.

"Yes I'll have Mr Burr lead you there," replies Ms Stephen.

"Hi I am Mr Burr," says Mr Burr

Mr Burr leads them to John and Kitty's living area

"I am Senator Jackson and this is my secretary Cecile. Have they told you your to be set free?" asks Andrew.

"I have noticed the train coming in is empty, it is no longer black; people are only exiting that is about it they don't tell us much of anything here. They quit making us do RT , and having to sign accountability roster. They made us working at the dining hall voluntary on basic wage," says Mr Burr.

Were you sent here for not paying your health insurance," asks Andrew.

"No sir I have been here for political reasons," replies Mr Burr.

"Your the fellow that John wrote to me about. Your free now everyone is to evacuate this place," says Andrew

"It's Senator Jackson John. Did I hear we are free," says Kitty and hugs Senator Jackson.

"Yes Kitty this place is to be evacuated and destroyed. This is my secretary Cecile. you can call me Andrew," says Andrew.

It is a glorious event, liberty, Andrew thank you for helping us," says John he shakes Andrew's hand and hugs him.

"There is a scorpion on the wall!" screams Cecile.

"That was the reaction I got when I first got here," says Kitty chuckling.

"Kitty your pregnant how wonderful. When are you expecting? asks Andrew.

"I am expecting triplets in December," answers Kitty

"Pack your stuff up and lets exit this creepy place," says Andrew.

John kills the scorpion and puts it in the trash.

"That's what I think of socialism, in the trash," says John

They all chuckle and start packing to leave for home. John and Kitty pack all their personal belongings.

"Kitty you have enough to carry ,with you being pregnant, we will take your stuff," says Andrew.

They all exit the new target of the Air Force after the building is evacuated, and board the helicopter. Andrew paid for the charter, this is a personal trip *Music, Chariots of Fire*

They leave the desolate desert of Nevada for the lush green lawns of Riverdale Tennessee. They are finally bound for home "Sweet Home" ☺.

Andrew, Cecile, John and Kitty check in the Bed and Breakfast in Riverdale to work on the damage that the government did and fix the mess they are in from being sent to the internment camp. There are many families that were sent to the internment camp that are in the same predicament when they get home like John and Kitty. We have to stay on this case of John and Kitty.

John calls the foster home to take back custody of their children. He also calls Uncle Billy.

"Mrs. Stivasant this is John Kadiddlehopper Kitty and myself are in Riverdale and we want our children back," says John on the phone.

" I will have them ready to leave at 2 PM is that OK, welcome home," replies Mrs. Stivasant on the phone.

"Yes that is fine we will see you at 2PM?" says John

"Billy we are back we need to pick up our van are you going to be home at one PM?" asks John on the phone.

"Sure Brother, we will have one grand family reunion when we are all together again. Where are you staying?" says Uncle Billy on the phone?

"We are staying at the Bed and Breakfast," replies John.

Immediately Uncle Billy acts as Paul Revere again, this time to report good news.

"Hello let me talk to the day reporter," says Uncle Billy to the KPOW receptionist.

"I will connect you," replies the KPOW receptionist.

"Hello are you interested John and Kitty Kadiddlehopper have been released from the internment camp?" asks Uncle Billy to the KPOW reporter.

"Sure are just tell us where and when to see them," replies the KPOW reporter.

"Meet them at the Bed and Breakfast at 4PM our family is together again," replies Uncle Billy.

"OK we will see you there," says the KPOW reporter.

Andrew takes John and Kitty to Uncle Billy's place and meets them back at the Bed and Breakfast.

John and Kitty pick the children from the foster home in the van after picking it up at Uncle Billy's.

"Mom Dad," says Arnold, Billy and Beatrice all together.

Family hugs and kisses all around.

"We missed you it is great to see your back with us," says Arnold

"Mom your pregnant, that's super," says Beatrice.

"I am expecting triplets in December," replies Kitty.

They go to their gas station to see what the situation is. John checks things out to see what is needed.

They find some inappropriate remarks on a fence, that is about it.

He gets back to the van.

"We can sell gas again and we have to order new stock for the food items eventually. Clean the place up wash the windows and the floor we will be back in business in a few days for selling gas. We are lucky they have not ordered us to remove our gas tanks out of the ground for us being out of business. Arnold I am going to need your help your going to have to work more your mother is in no condition to work now.

They drive to the bed and breakfast, and sit out on the front porch and Andrew and Cecile join them.

"Andrew this is Arnold, Beatrice and Billy," says Kitty.

"Thank you Andrew for helping mom and dad come home, you deserve the name OLE Hickory," says Beatrice.

"Yeah OLE Hickory," says Billy. shakes Andrew's hand.

"For sure OLE Hickory," says Arnold shakes Andrew's hand.

The KPOW News reporter arrives at the Bed and Breakfast.

"I am looking for John and Kitty," says the KPOW reporter.

"Your looking at them," says John.

They are being on video now.

"Senator Jackson what a pleasant surprise. It is nice to meet you all. John so how soon are you going to be back in business?" asks the KPOW reporter.

"In three days We will be selling gas only. It will be a while till we are selling food and drinks and related items. We have to order all new stock for the store," replies John.

"Kitty I see your pregnant," says the KPOW reporter.

"I am expecting triplets in December," says Kitty

"Where are you staying now after your stay here?" asks the KPOW reporter.

"Right now temporarily we are staying at my brother in laws. Our house was foreclosed a few months after we were sent to the internment camp so I guess we have to find another place," replies Kitty.

"Would you want your old place back," asks the KPOW reporter.

"Yes it would be wonderful if it happen," replies Kitty and John nods yes.

"Senator Jackson what brings you to Riverdale," asks the KPOW reporter.

"I am here to help John and Kitty get home sooner than is scheduled. If they had to wait it would not be till the train of Liberty was scheduled to take them home it would be a month later. I have to work on a plan for reparations to the former residents that stayed at the federal internment camp that does not come out of the government budget. I leave for Washington tomorrow," says Andrew.

"OLE Hickory working for us, he truly is a champion working on our side," says the KPOW reporter starts to pack up and leave.

"Dinner is ready!" yells Beatrice.

They all head for the dinner table with John at the head of the table.

"Kitty and myself would like to make a announcement everyone. We would like to make Andrew and Cecile godparents when the triplets are born," says John.

They all eat dinner after saying grace.

"I would consider that a honor," says Andrew.

"Me too," says Cecile.

"I just realized we have a problem with health insurance with me expecting. No insurance company will take me now," says Kitty

"Contact the local mid wife services, and apply for Medicaid if you have complications if the babies are in the wrong position upon birth. That way you only have to rely on the government for just a emergency," suggests Cecile.

" I like that idea we will look into getting a midwife for my pregnancy," says Kitty.

"This roast is really yummy," says Arnold.

"I love the mash potatoes," says Billy

" This scrumptious pecan pie, I ate first," says Beatrice.

"Coming home the food situation we have to go to the food bank to get restocked up until the gas station gets back up to speed," says John

"Don't be too proud to apply for food stamps, children eat a lot of food. The government put you in the situation your in. Andrew made a point not to cut food stamps when we presented the Kadiddlehopper Bill to congress says Cecile.

"Andrew what do you have planned after you go to Washington?" asks John.

"I have to do some personal business and make good on a promise. I think you will all like that promise. Keep a close watch on TV and the Internet," says Andrew.

"What was it like you Filibustering the senate OLE Hickory?" asks Billy.

"It was one of the hardest things I have ever done Billy. I now hold the record of 25 hours Filibustering, talking the whole time. I fainted tough I hope I don't have to do that again to get a bill passed," replies Andrew.

"When I grow up I want to be a Senator like OLE Hickory. says Billy.

"Andrew you have a fan," says Kitty.

"Andrew is our hero mom he liberated you and dad from that dreadful place" says Beatrice.

"Well with that positive remark, Cecile and I have a long day traveling back to Washington. It has been very special to me to meet Arnold, Beatrice and Billy. I will see you all soon when the triplets are born," says Andrew.

Eventually everyone went to bed. That night the news got out that John and Kitty are back in Riverdale.

The next morning John took off to work and the children went to school. Andrew and Cecile checked out to take off to Washington. Kitty slept in, and she planned to check out of the bed and Breakfast check out time, and go to Billy's place to live.

"I am looking for ether John and Kitty," says the bank loan officer.

"I'll get Kitty" replies the Bed and Breakfast host.

Kitty comes to meet him.

"Hi Kitty I have some great news! Did you hear the evening news last night?

No I did not, I get sleepy often, pregnant you know," replies Kitty.

"Well there was overwhelming donations from the community to completely pay off your house early this morning. The bank president took your house out of foreclosure, and I have right here the deed to your house paid in full. I need for you to sign right here," says the bank loan officer.

Kitty signs the receipt of the deed.

"Oh thank you so much," says Kitty almost in tears of happiness.

"I will be on my way, I am sure you have lots of work to do," says the bank loan officer.

"Bye thank you," says Kitty waving.

Kitty gets on phone to spread the news

"Guess what just happen?" asks Kitty to John the phone.

"We won 10 million dollars," answers John.

"No, think family dear," replies Kitty. *pause*

"Oh my god, we got the our house back," says John.

"You got it, a bank officer came and we own the house free and clear. I have the deed right here. All we have to do is pay the property taxes," says Kitty.

"I'll close up here and pick you up to go home. Thank God, he defiantly loves us" says John.

"Thank all of Riverdale they are the best honey" says Kitty.

John picked Kitty up and they saw their house like it was condition like a episode of The Twilight Zone or a horror movie. The lawn expectedly needed mowing and is three feet high. Some of the shutters were hanging on only one hinge. When they got inside everything has not been touched from the day the IRS arrested them. Cob webs everywhere that could easily be cleaned up.

"In a few days honey we will have this place normal again. So hold me tight dear it will be all right," says John slow dancing with Kitty.

Music "Oh what a Feeling", Boston

So as soon as the children got the news about the house, they came home, and pitched in to get it in shape. Arnold, and Billy mowed the lawn and Beatrice cleaned up the house. John fixed the shingles and went to get a huge banner red ,white, and blue banner that was long enough to completely go across the front of the house. The banner says "Thank you Riverdale Your the Best,". After the banner is up Kitty gets the tripod out and takes a picture of all of them in front of the house.

"Say Jabberwalkie," says Kitty.

Then they emailed the picture to Andrew and the Press, Home Sweet Home!

Chapter Ten

A symbol of Socialism Dies
Faith, Hope, and Charity in Washington

When Andrew got back to Washington he got a message from Major General Arnold that "The Stage is Set". He called him back and made a appointment and arranged to be there the day after all the residents of the internment camp have been evacuated That is the day before Thanksgiving. So he called the press corps to be there to watch, and took a plane with Cecile back to the site of the internment camp that is five miles away from the site to view the event.

"General is everything ready?" asks Andrew.

"Yes Senator we are testing our new B2010 and the Juggernaught smart bomb that is the biggest non nuclear bomb to date. I appreciate this testing site we mostly have just desert holes in the ground," replies General Arnold.

"General the American people thank you, this site is remote I figured it be a good target. Keep your cameras on that building, " says Andrew to the general and the press.

The forward air traffic controller contacts the bomber controller the location.

They can't hear the B2010 and see a plane in the sky.

Music "The Danger Zone" Kenny Loggins

The bomber releases it's bombs the concussion is like a volcano blowing it's top in a huge mushroom cloud the three floor brick building, scorpions, tarantulas, and bats infested, is reduced to one big hole in the ground. The press is in awe the shear power of the juggernaught bombs.

"It was a successful bombing," says General Arnold.

"It is what Americans do BEST with it's Air Force, and promise I made is kept," says Andrew smiling!

"That is for sure Senator," says General Arnold. chuckling.

"Yes!" reacted Joan Jenson watching TV.

"Senator Jackson what is your thoughts about the bombing?" asks ROX News.

"The children of our country do not have to worry again about being sent to this place that was a result of socialism," replies Senator Jackson.

Andrew departed to Washington to finish some business about the former internment camp residents.

Back at the capitol in the hall Andrew sees Bill (Senator Cranberry).

"Hi Bill do you have a minute," asks Andrew?

"Yes what is it," replies Bill.

"I would like to have a meeting with you concerning the former internment camp residents" asks Andrew.

"Would 1 PM tomorrow in my office be OK?" asks Bill.

"That will be fine you have a good day," responds Andrew.

The next afternoon Andrew is in Bill's office.

"I am here to see Senator Cranberry," says Andrew.

"Yes he is expecting you," replies his secretary.

" It's good to see you please enlighten me OLE Hickory what do you propose about the former internment camp residents?" asks Bill.

"The former residents of the internment camp have been displaced by the government. I was wondering if you would help me soliciting for non government donations so they can get there lives back together," asks Andrew

"I like that idea some charity work and good public relations. We can ask for donations in front of the Lincoln Memorial and invite the press," replies Bill.

"I will have Cecile invite them for a press conference on the steps weather permitting," says Andrew.

I'll do the same what day?" asks Bill.

Friday after our senate session. I have one other thing to discuss" replies Andrew.

"What is it about?" asks Bill.

" I have been trying to locate Myrna with no success do you have a address for me to work on locating Paul?" asks Andrew.

"All I have is this address Mr Petabone gave me," responds Bill and looks for the address and gives it to Andrew.

"Thanks, this gives me something to work on," says Andrew.

Friday afternoon on the steps of the Lincoln Memorial Senators Jackson and Cranberry held a press conference.

"The former residents of the federal internment camp need your help for as little as a dollar you can help them put their lives together. Log on www.helplives.com

I put the government on a strict budget and there is no funds for a appropriation," says Senator Jackson.

"Your help will help them get new places to live, and new health insurance and to

readjust from being torn from normal life to a place socialism built," says Senator Cranberry.

The donations poured in and the charity work of both senators is a complete success. It helped the former residents of the internment camp get back in the main stream of life, and made the transition much easier.

ROX News reports this special report.

"We are in Paris, France, the Tennessee tycoon Earnest Peabody wanted by the FBI

has been arrested and will be extradited back to the USA," reports ROX news.

After that the Senate went on a holiday break

Chapter Eleven

The personal life of Senator Jackson

In the car, parked Andrew called Cecile.

"You want to go out to dinner tonight?" asks Andrew to Cecile on the phone.

"Sounds good I have nothing planned," replies Cecile on the phone.

Andrew drove to Cecile's place and knocked on the door they kissed and got in the car.

"I have a place to take you it is on the way," says Andrew driving.

"That's cool where to honey," asks Cecile?

"You will see," says Andrew.

They drive to the Jackson Memorial and get out and they sit on a bench.

Andrew half knees in front of Cecile

"Cecile picture us in a light house and the sea was all the women in the world.

None of them matter to me just you.

I love you and our love is inside the love triangle and I want to spend the rest of our life together. Will you marry me?" asks Andrew and gives the ring.

Cecile thinks with a long pause.

"Yes I will marry you," replies Cecile and kisses Andrew

"We have to get going to dinner, I am so happy," says Andrew.

"No first I want to try something I learned in college," says Cecile

She takes her ring and scratches the base of the monument.

"It's real if it was cubic zirconium it would not scratch it," says Cecile

"I spent a mint on that ring," says Andrew.

"Relax dear nothing can harm a diamond exempt another diamond," says Cecile

"OK you had your experiment lets go. You know quartz would scratch cement too but it does have a tendency to crack when hit right. If you were careful you would never know the difference," says Andrew.

"Until you rap it against something and it cracks into little tiny pieces, I'd rather have real diamonds," says Cecile.

"Lets go to dinner we had our Geology 101 experiment today," says Andrew.

"I am for steak and lobster, lets start our engagement in style," says Cecile.

"Sure that sounds good, your the expert for restaurants in this town," replies Andrew.

They both get in the car and drive.

"So what it is the best place for lobster?" asks Andrew.

"Granny's Maine Lobster, we will be approaching it on the right," says Cecile.

They drive in, park, and walk in.

"We like a table for two," says Andrew.

They get seated and the waiter greets them.

" May I take your order or do you want to look first. Our Steak and lobster is on special tonight," says Ralph the waiter.

"I'll have the special, with ice tea, and steak medium well done," says Andrew

"I'll have the same," says Cecile.

The waiter leaves them alone.

"So how soon do you want to get married?" asks Andrew.

"Soon as we can make arrangements; I don't want a big wedding just basic and simple. A big honeymoon like Paris," says Cecile.

"That would not be good for public relations. Niagara Falls would be better then we go to Paris later when I am not a senator. I have some personal business in Nashville.

We can get married in front of the Hermitage in Nashville," says Andrew

" I like that idea, who do you have to see in Nashville," asks Cecile

"For my son, I have a address I have to follow up on to see if he is there, we can get our marriage license there too," says Andrew.

"How soon do we leave for Nashville," asks Cecile?

"Tomorrow afternoon we leave for Nashville," replies Andrew.

"I have your order," says Ralph the waiter.

They crack the lobster open and start to eat dinner.

"This is good lobster, you pick out great places to eat dear," says Andrew.

She chuckles:

"Wait till you feel what happens when we are done," says Cecile.

"So have you thought how big a family you want" asks Andrew?

"I want a huge family with our children all over the house. You know Teddy Roosevelt had nine children. One after another as long as I am able to have them with you," says Cecile.

"The Jackson family population explosion is about to begin. Procreation for us is the only way," says Andrew.

"Finnish your dinner, dear, and take me home, the anticipation is getting unbearable" says Cecile

They ate dinner and Andrew took her home. They get to the door.

"Your coming in aren't you," says Cecile.

"I have a problem," says Andrew☺.

"Well come on in you sexy, spicy man, and I will take care of your problem. "When I am Good I am Very Good, when I am bad I am Better," *(Mae West, I am No Angel, 1933)* says Cecile in a sexy voice and takes Andrew's hand to lead him in the house☺.

Music, "Take my Breath Away" Berlin

The day after in the afternoon Andrew and Cecile flew to Nashville Tennessee and rented a car. They went to the court house and got a marriage license and contacted a local pastor, Father Mc Carthy. They are in his rectory talking to him.

"We have our marriage license we like you to marry us right away," says Andrew.

"Have you known each other for over 6 months?" asks father Mc Carthy.

"Seven months father," Cecile.

"Where do want to get married, in the church here?" asks father Mc Carthy.

"At the Hermitage Father," replies Andrew.

"I can say a short mass, and marry you on Thursday at one PM at the Hermitage is that OK?" asks father Mc Carthy.

"That will be fine father; we thank you on such short notice," says Andrew.

In the time Andrew and Cecile are to wait to get married they checked out the address that Andrew has to find his son. They get to the address and turns out to be a transitional housing facility

At the front desk they see a social worker.

"Is Boom, Boom, Myrna staying here I'm Senator Andrew Jackson V?" asks Andrew.

"Yes she is, I will go get her," says the social worker.

By surprise Andrew sees, Stephanie, Earnest Peabody's ex secretary walking by.

"Stephanie how did you end up here, this my wife to be Cecile?" asks Andrew.

"That louse Earnest Peabody dropped me off here before he got sent to Fort Leavenworth for 20 years," replies Stephanie.

"Well I am sort of responsible for you being here," says Andrew.

"Stephanie we are getting married Thursday, Andrew told me what you think of him. I need a maid of honor on Thursday at the Hermitage. Will you be my maid of honor?   Andrew will need a new secretary and I am willing to teach you. I will be too busy with our family," says Cecile.

"I'd love be your maid of honor, and I get to spend time with Andrew Baby. I'd love to be his secretary. Aren't you going to be a little jealous of me," asks Stephanie?

"Not if I am the mother of his children. You have a important responsibility if some happens to me if I pass on performing childbirth. It sounds morbid, it is really very practical. I need a mid wife very soon too. I have not told Andrew yet I am pregnant with his child. It will be one of many; we plan to have a big family.

"Then settled your my maid of honor, midwife and Andrew's secretary.

Cecile chats with Stephanie for awhile when he is talking with Myrna.

"Andrew what are you doing here?" asks Myrna.

"You have not told me about Paul Myrna. I found out the hard way in a Senate ethics committee hearing. Can I see my son?" asks Andrew.

"I'm sorry you found out that way, and I am relived that you know the truth now. As you can see I am not in the best situation to take care of him now," says Myrna.

"I want Paul to finally know his father, and be the son I always wanted.

I am willing to get you a place to stay, and Paul can see you any time he wants. He will stay with me until we establish some emotional bonding," says Andrew.

"He needs to be with his dad, and I love to get out of this place. I will go get him," says Myrna.

I feel like to get something to eat; Cecile and Stephanie what do you want?" asks Andrew.

"Paul I'd like you to meet your father. Honey I am sorry I never told you have a dad. I never told him he has a son up to just recently he found out. He loves you very much to be here," says Myrna

" I saw you on TV, cool my dad is OLE Hickory" says Paul he hugs his dad too.

"He sure is honey he is your dad," says Myrna.

"Paul what do you want to eat. You can have anything you want?" asks Andrew.

"There is a hamburger place around the cornier, I want hamburgers, it's called Teddy's Hamburger's," says Paul.

"Well lets all go to Teddy's," says Andrew.

So Andrew, Cecile, Stephanie, Myrna and Paul all went out to lunch and went in and the are seated. They order what the want to eat.

"Myrna I'd like for you to be a bridesmaid on Thursday for our wedding," says Cecile.

"Myrna I'd like that, all one happy family," says Myrna.

"Do you have a place that you have in mind to move to Myrna?" asks Andrew.

"There is a trailer and it's on a small lot I have in mind that is for sale" replies Myrna.

"I will buy that trailer for you and the lot all you have to do is pay for property taxes , and utilities; we will help you move too," says Andrew.

"How soon will that happen?" asks Myrna.

"Tomorrow I will contact the Realtor or owner to make a fast sale, then we will move you in, no more transitional hosing," says Andrew.

"I see what you mean Cecile, Andrew Baby takes care of this own. He is the best, and very responsible," says Stephanie.

"That will be great to have my own place," says Myrna.

"Good hamburger dad, thanks," says Paul.

"I have a announcement to make I am two months pregnant" says Cecile.

"Great news Cecile, Myrna, Paul is staying with us and you can too until we get you a place tomorrow. Then we can help move you in the new place" says Andrew.

After lunch they all stayed overnight at Andrew's place. Andrew and Myrna located the Realtor and arranged a quick deed on the trailer and lot. That afternoon they moved Myrna in her new trailer.   Andrew and Cecile are getting ready for their wedding in front of the Hermitage. Andrew made sure that Cecile would be able to have her wedding cake and had the cake baker make a brides layer just for her.

Father Mc Carthy said mass, and then proceeded to marry Andrew and Cecile with Stephanie, Myrna and Paul

The wedding vows:

"Andrew do you take this woman Cecile Smitherpoo to be your lawful wedded wife. In sickness or health, richer or poor until DEATH do you part?" asks Father Mc Carthy.

"I do," replies Andrew.

"Cecile do you take this man Andrew Jackson V to be your lawful husband. In sickness and in health, Richer or poorer, until Death do you part?" asks Father Mc Carthy.

"I do," replies Cecile.

"You may exchange rings," says Father Mc Carthy.

"With this ring I thee wed with honor and devotion," says Andrew he puts the ring on Cecile's finger.

"With this ring I thee wed my beloved husband," says Cecile she puts the ring on Andrews finger.

"Is there anyone that objects to Andrew and Cecile being wed speak now or forever hold your peace *(pause)*? Then the power invested in me and the state of Tennessee I pronounce Mr and Mrs. Andrew Jackson V. You way kiss the bride Andrew," says Father Mc Carthy.

Andrew and Cecile kiss one long kiss, and have small reception too.

(Music: The power of love)

(If you believe in paranormal Andrew Jackson is smiling in the distance)

After they are married, Andrew and Cecile took Stephanie back to Washington to work at his office while they were off on their honeymoon. Andrew thought of the weather in Niagara Falls in the winter, in December, the ice is starting to flow down the river and the Maid of the Mist and Cave of the Winds will be closed down until the ice melts in June. They also have Paul now with them on their honeymoon. It is a better alternative than leave him with some one. Paul got some much needed emotional bonding with his father.

So they decided to go to St. Thomas for their honeymoon; the threesome had fun in the sun. It is still in the USA so off and away they went.

Chapter Twelve

Delivery of Three Little Miracles
The Final Struggle

Andrew, Paul, and Cecile after a most enjoyable honeymoon flew back to Washington;

Andrew is very much pleased how Stephanie is taken charge in the office, and she is doing very well. The news that Kitty will have her triplets near Christmas is received; Andrew and Cecile fly to Riverdale, Tennessee for the new godparents to be present when the triplets are born. The Jackson's check in the Bed and Breakfast and are there through New Years Day.

Kitty's midwife is getting things ready for the delivery; John is getting hyped about coaching Kitty threw the long marathon of labor. It is her heroic struggle for the family survival that makes all what they have been through worth while.

It is the 23rd of December and everyone is getting ready for the Christmas to remember.

In the morning, The Kadiddlehopper family is sitting at the breakfast table as usual. The have the morning news on TV.

"We bring you this special report. Tennessee Governor Milton Hornblower has announced that Thaddeus Smith has been appointed as a new senator that replaces impeached former senator John Petabone," reports ROX news on TV.

"Mr Smith Goes to Washington sounds good☺," says John.

"Dad where is the orange juice." asks Billy opening the refrigerator door?

"It's on the top shelf as usual," replies John

Billy finds the orange juice and takes it to the table.

"Mr Smith wasn't that a movie Dad?" asks Beatrice.

"Yes dear, Mr Smith Goes to Washington was directed by Frank Capra in 1939. He also directed, You can't take it with you," replies John.

"Meet John Doe too, dad, I like the part he gave away twenty million dollars to people, and the tycoons had a fit in court," says Arnold.

"I hope we can see, It's a Wonderful Life, this Christmas, I liked that about Clarence the angel getting his wings," says Beatrice.

"What is so great about really old movies?" asks Billy.

"Some of those, really old movies, as you call them, can teach you a valuable lesson," replies John.

"Lost Horizon, that is a cool movie, they get kidnapped to this land called Sangria LA that is somewhere in the mountains, and they never get old when your there," says Arnold.

The talk about the movies John, Arnold, Billy and Beatrice went on watching a Frank Capra movie binge to pass the time. Kitty is eating and sleeping in bed and is being taken care of by her midwife Mrs. Katzjammer.

Later that night, just before midnight, Mrs. Katzjammer runs in the living room where they are watching movies.

"Kitty's water broke, please hurry John it's happening," says Mrs. Katzjammer.

"Arnold you call the Jackson's, Billy you call your Uncle Billy, Beatrice I need your help," says John.

John and Beatrice rush into the bedroom that Kitty is to give birth.

"Breath just like we practiced dear, deep breaths, hold my arms, if have claw marks on my arms, I'll wear them as a proud father. Beatrice cuddle with your mom it makes her produce a hormone called Oxytocin that helps some to relieve the pain" says John.

Andrew, Cecile, Arnold, Billy, and Uncle Billy come in the room Cecile cuddles with Kitty. Paul is watching TV in the living room.

"Andrew we are all here to help you get though this," says Andrew.

"Are there any complications Mrs. K?" asks John.

"She is doing fine John," replies Mrs. K.

Kitty has a labor pains and they are getting more frequent.

About a hour later the first of the three start the journey to life.

"I can see the head we are doing fine PUSH Kitty," says Mrs. K.

"PUSH MOM," says Beatrice.

"ERRR Screaming," Yells Kitty her finger nails are gouging John's arms.

"It's coming PUSH, Come on Kitty almost there," says Mrs. K.

"YEEE AHHH," yells Kitty.

"It's A BOY," says Mrs. K she takes care of the umbilical cord, slaps him, and gives him to Beatrice to wash off and put in a blanket; she gives Kitty some water.

"That's Andrew," says John.

Beatrice holds Little Andrew until the other two are born.

"I see a head Kitty push second one on the way," says Mrs. K

"Push MOM," says Beatrice.

"PUSH Kitty," says John.

"EEEEAH SCREAMING," yells Kitty clawing John's arms to the bone, and they are a bloody mess.

"PUSH Kitty it's Coming, Come One more, PUSH," says Mrs. K.

"DAMM YOU JOHN, I AM NOT GOING THREW THIS AGAIN," screams Kitty. John's arms are now just as bad off than Kitty's pain.

"COME ON DEAR PUSH, BREATH DEEP WE WILL GET through this.

Billy get something for my arms," says John.

Billy gets a towel from the bathroom.

"It's coming PUSH, COMING, PUSH, that's it. There we go, it's a girl," says Mrs. K she takes care of the umbilical cord and gives her a slap and gives her to Cecile.

"Third one should come out like grease lighting. That's Little Cecile, Cecile," says John.

"One more Kitty PUSH," says Mrs. K.

"URRAH SCREAMING!" YELLS Kitty.

"ONE more PUSH come on" says Mrs. K. she gives Kitty some water.

"RRREEEAH SCREAMING, GREASE LIGHTING, JOHN, MY ASS, this one is just as painful!" yells Kitty.

"This is the finish line, PUSH KITTY, PUSH," says Mrs. K.

"URRRAHSH SCREAMS," yells Kitty.

"PUSH Kitty, That's it, I got it, It's a boy, three little miracles Kitty, you and John are truly blessed☺" says Mrs. K. she takes care of the umbilcal cord slaps him and gives him to Kitty to nurse him.

"YES, this is John Jr." says John

"Paul get in here for your picture taken with the babies," says Andrew

Kitty holds the other two while Mrs. K takes the picture of everyone, "The Family Prevails,". Then they all sing Silent Night and God Bless Amercia.

The End

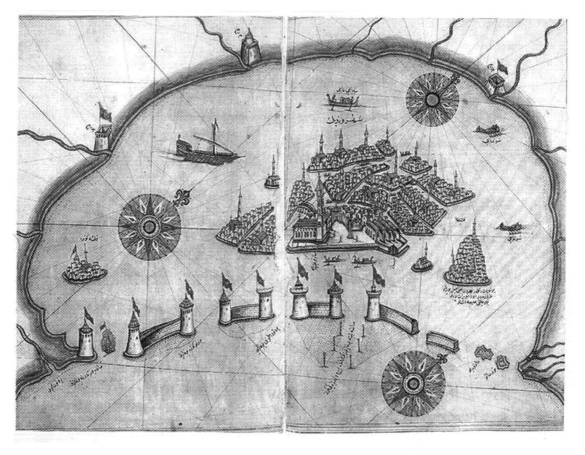

50

Epilogue

Things To Remember

Chapter two is the metaphor the demonstration signs being smashed against the paddy wagon that is government property. It is illegal to destroy government property. I can get away writing about it, DON'T do it for real. It signifies the frustration not listening to the people.

This story is fiction in the year 2015; there may be a instance a name of someone has been used in this story. The characters names are just part of this story nothing more. I am sure I have heighten the name Jackson though, and that is a good thing.

People may question what political party is Andrew Jackson V? He is American first, and the party you imagine him to be.

I do urge you to vote so places and things like internment camps, Death of Freedom Express never do exist. You may laugh at first, if nothing is said, then you might end up like John and Kitty. If you let the government get away for taxing or fining people for not paying health insurance who is going to stop them from going further. With socialism you get to the point there is not enough people to pay the taxes. The Soviet Union and Cuba have all ready tried socialism; I don't have to say a word what has happen to them.

In this story I gave you the dots and let your imagination fill in the blanks. I stayed razor sharp on the plot, and did not give you a lot of flowery dialog to put you to sleep. So what, this story is not a novel.

The emotion having triplets for real, must be really something. I want children, I am single, just writing about it like I was there was emotional for me. I am sure my experience is only one tenth the emotion to be blessed have three gifts from god come all at once. I think what a way to end a story, a wedding, and a triple birth with my creativity.

If this story becomes a movie it be most fitting it starts with the Death of Freedom Express with it's articulated steam locomotive, black flags, black baggage cars. It gets the message across this is the result of you not taking the time to vote and making your voice herd. OH YES the Air Force bombing the internment camp would make a great trailer. God Bless America, long may our flag wave!

William Quayle Jr.

References

You Can not Take it With You, directed by Frank Capra 1938

It's a Wonderful Life, Frank Capra 1941

Lost Horizon, Frank Capra 1936

Mr Smith goes to Washington, Frank Capra 1939

Meet John Doe, Frank Capra

I'm 1935no Angel, Mae West 1933

Iago's Victory
The Spectacle never ends!
Copyright TXu001644859 / 2009-07-31
copying this play/screenplay must have the written
permission from William Quayle Jr.
1/23/09

Synopsis:

Iago's Victory has a plot that has two sub plots. It starts like the familiar Shakespearean play Othello it is in new English and not old English with about one third the dialog. At the death of Othello William Shakespeare ends, and William Quayle's creativity starts. The audience will find their own hero from such a diverse cast in this screenplay.

The first mission is the Island of Cypress where the three tons of Minion gold is in a deep catacomb and they have to get to it. Getting to it is like Indiana Jones of the fourteenth century; for they have booby traps, creatures to kill like Fire spiders, glass dread spiders that make zombies, vampires, Giant rock men, Fire giants, a underground river to bridge and cross, vampires. Booby traps like, big huge rock rolling pin, Rolling rock, and ax gantlet. Huge explosions of the Turkish weapons cache. The capture of the Colossus cannon and the mad dash to the cove where the Byzantine and pirate fleets are.

There are several out of the box events to keep the audience wondering what will happen next like, sub plot, the five witches from no where. They later keep the Dread Black Knight from Masadonia from making it to the international jousting tournament, in the forest of thorns. The forest of thorns is a symbolic representation of poverty, how it keeps a person from doing what they want. The Othello's Handkerchief is not just any handkerchief it's enchanted. It made Desdemona make the mistake of marring Othello. Magic is a dominant existence in this screenplay. It does have its finding away home moments when the Desdemona gives the caldron from her fathers service in the Crusades. The witches use the caldron to get home.

Main characters like Cassio and Ruth the Ruthless Pirate are the first couple. Casanova the parrot is defiantly a hero. He saves Cassio, Ruth and crews, more than once.

The second mission and climax, is the defense of Venice.

It has a little romance Desdemona asks Iago to be her champion and the last act he follows threw with that promise. Iago really gets two victory's in this screenplay for one he gets Desdemona's hand and wins the battle of Venice. Ruth and Cassio are promoted to admiral and they prove their expertise in the battle.

Rodegro leads the most formidable Catapracts in the world to hit and run of 5000 gunpowder Jannesarys that have hand cannons. There is also the battle the Jannesarys setting siege the walls of Venice, This is the grand spectacle of this movie the battle.

I never seen a battle with hand cannons this movie is another first. Barbantio's stand at his keep and his death, keeping the Jannesarys from going no further into the city. His death will make anyone tear up. Desdemona crying over his body. They make a monument in his honor the defender of Venice. The sight of Ruth manning the Colossus cannon with Casanova on the wall is also a key scenes.

The battle of Venice that is the epic climax has naval battles never before seen on screen.

Greek fire was used by the Byzantine navy and we get to see why they still used it. It is like spewing Napalm and the effect is devastating. They also had double hulls that made them almost unsinkable. A few sink and they are out numbered three to four to one.

The third mission is the international jousting tournament. This is where the shivery runs amuck. The clanking of swords, armor and shields; Fourteenth century gladiators keeps the audience on the edge.

Iago convinces the duke they should celebrate their victory over the Turks by holding a jousting tournament. Knights from all over the world compete including Ruth the Ruthless pirate. By surprise a lot of knights discover they just been defeated by a woman.

Peril , Rodergo, Desdemona, Iago, Ruth and Cassio have a triple wedding. The screenplay ends up in the Venice Cathedral , wedding, with pomp and a lot of merry music. By far this screenplay has been written in the Hollywood style.

Marketing: The marketing of this screenplay is like the Star Wars or Indiana Jones of **the fourteenth century**. It is nothing like ether one; that is just to give you the idea of how big this can be. Sales of memorabilia like Ruth the Ruthless pirate . She is as dominant as wonder woman or Xena. Casanova, Cassio, Barbantio, Rodrego, Othello. If Marketed right should make the production of this screenplay a "Blockbuster epic". AND HUGE Profits. It has international appeal not just in the USA.

The key is take out the risk of the production. When I write it is the I think of the big picture then write the dialog to it. Animation is defiantly a option with the sea battles, the catacombs and the Janessary attacks. Computer animation is needed much of this screenplay. This is not just a movie, it's a franchise and all that goes with the movie.

Cast for screenplay: Scene one and two.
 Barbantio
 Iago
 Roderigo
 DESDEMONA
 Othello (Does not have to be a black American)
 Crystol
 Othello's Gypsy Mother
 Barbantio's squire
 First Swiss Pikeman
 Second Swiss Pikeman
 Third Swiss Pikeman
 Forth Swiss Pikeman
 Fifth Swiss Pikeman
 White witch Andrella *from the land of Ozone the most powerful witch Like the witch from the north in Oz*
 Blue witch Barbella *from the land of Ozone*
 Tizzy witch *from the play Macbeth Blond Hair*
 Lizzy witch *from the play Macbeth Red Hair*
 Dizzy *witch from the play Macbeth Brunette hair*

Seine one

Play opens with DESDEMONA running out of the balcony laden house with suitcase.

Iago

to Roderigo
front of house in Venice A Street
It is a wonderful day, Who was that running out of that house Roderigo.

Roderigo

It is Othello's new bride *DESDEMONA*

Iago

I did not know Othello got married.

Roderigo

It was all of a sudden like Othello had a magic spell upon her.

Iago

I wonder how he managed that, every wealthy single male in Venice, has tried to get Desdemona's
hand.

Roderigo

He did not even ask her father for her hand they eloped.

Iago

What do you think how her father would react such a Life time commitment without his consent.

Roderigo:

This is his house let summon him and ask him about his daughter where she has gone.

Iago

Yell's up to the balcony Sir Barbantio do you know were your daughter has gone.

Barbantio:

What is this thief, Who are you.

Roderigo:

I'm Roderigo, is your daughter in the house?
Barbantio *Looks in her bedroom she is not there. Comes back to the balcony.*
I have looked all over the house no my daughter has fled my
love, and my protection.

Iago

Mr Roderigo and myself saw her running from your house this morning, Brabaintio.

Barbantio:
Do you know whom she has ran to without a word to me?

Roderigo:
I am sorry to inform you your daughter has eloped to the Moor Othello. She is married to him.

Barbantio
angry
Where can I confront this THEIF Othello!

Iago
He is my commander and I can summon him for military matters.

Barbantio:
yelling
Squire get my chain mail we are to arrest this thief Othello. Iago please summon him and meet me at the Venice City Square as soon as possible. Squire call my pikemen and make it quick as well after you get my armor and my trusty broad sword and shield. We must confront Othello tonight!

Roderigo:
I do not think anyone told Othello you were a retired knight, veteran of the Crusades, Knights Templar. You're a senator as well. I will summon your pikemen as well.

Barbantio:
It is our advantage he does not know I have been a well decorated knight in the Byzantine army, veteran of the Crusades. I am the holder of the trusted CROSS of the Byzantine army. If he resists arrest it will be at his peril. It will be Othello's last battle! Roderigo tell my pikemen be prepared for intense battle.

Seine Two

Venice City Square
Brabaintio *Arrives at the Venice City Square in full armor with a huge red Cross on his armor.*
Roderigo is my pikemen ready?
Roderigo *Marches Five elite Swiss pikemen into the Venice City square.*
Five pikemen are ready for your orders sir.
Othello enters the scene to the middle of the Venice City Square.

Iago
Sir Barbantio it is the Moor Othello
Barbantio STOP Othello you thief.
Draws broad sword.

Othello *Draws sword.*
Put away that sword old man your age, does you better, than your prowess with that sword.

Iago

Othello sir you may be my commander, Sir Barbantio is not just any old man. He has been in the last Crusades and is a excellent swordsman.

Roderigo

Othello you are in for a nasty surprise .   I have seen Sir Barbantio's house he is no ordinary old man. He is a retired Knights Templar.

Othello

I have taken many men the likes of him, with the same odds as in this square.

Barbantio:

Ready to engage Othello sword drawn.
You sacrilegious, wretched swine where is my daughter.
For you have charmed her with magic and clouded her sense of reason.
For this act has me asking myself why this has happen.
My daughter as beautiful as she is and envy of all the women in Venice.
She has kept the rich suitors of Venice at bay. None of them she has considered for marriage. You have made the men of our city look like they are second class. In reality they are the cream of society. Instead she has run away from my love and protection, to a unworthy, ugly, dirty, suitor. You have swayed her reason with forceful foreplay and rape. Drugged her with marijuana and strong drinks.
For this makes no sense to me at all. I wonder if she acted on her own and you made love to her.
Marriage is the only out for her to avoid embarrassment with the city of Venice.
I therefore put you in the state of arrest
For if you resist it will be your last battle, and certain death.

All Pikemen

Othello to the witness stand, Othello to the witness stand. We will fry him like a batter cake when we get him where we want him.
Roderigo *bats all pikemen hits helmet.*
You lame brains that dialog is for another play.

Othello

sword drawn
I have killed many men, old man. I reject your act to arrest me.

Barbantio

Then we will fight you fool. You will face hell and certain death of your very soul.
Pikemen surround Othello if he engages you kill him. *Heavy melee fighting to death! Sound of sword fighting.*

Iago:

while heavy theater combat heavy melee fighting. At least five minutes.
Directors discretion of combat

General this act is foolish. You are outnumbered six to one these are not just ordinary pikemen. They are Swiss pikemen missionaries

Roderigo:
General you are engaging a knight that has more kills than yourself stop this foolishness.

Othello:
while fighting
I have fought with such odds as these and won.

Barbantio:
while fighting
You will get no undertaker in this city. You will be skewered like a pin cushion and hung face down in the Venice City Square. PIKEMEN lunge forward engage Othello.
Othello: *gets stabbed by three pikemen bleeding. Heavy melee fighting surrounded by pikemen. Fighting to death* We will see about that.

Barbantio:
with no place to go Barbantio makes a killing cut is right arm completely off. Kills Othello. He castrates Othello the second swipe of his blade. Blood is everywhere.

Iago:
Othello was warned he was foolish to engage you.
Sir you just gave me a promotion Sir Barbantio. Thank you.

Barbantio:
Checks body… Put this handkerchief over Othello's eyes may he never lay eyes on a Venetian woman again. Hang him head facing down. *Leaves stage.*
Pikemen hang Othello in Venice City Square. After they hang him, two Pikemen stand guard.
Rest exit stage,
brief silence.
All of a sudden a green and white pouf of smoke near the body of Othello.
At the same time five witches appear

All five witches
Were are we.

Tizzy to Dizzy *to*
Andrella
This is the wrong play looks like… Is that Othello? Were not in Macbeth anymore Dizzy just what did you put in that spell. I told you put a chickens foot in the ingredients. Looks like we are in Venice instead of London.

Same time as Tizzy
Andrella
Barbella were not in Ozone anymore. This looks like Venice.

Look is that Othello? One of the Macbeth witches must have made us appear here.
Look a enchanted handkerchief that is on Othello. Those pikemen are guarding him.

Dizzy
to Tizzy
I put a rabbits foot in the ingredients must have also said the wrong words. Bubble double, trouble. We all want to go to London bubble.

Tizzy, Lizzy, Andrella, Barbella.
To Dizzy
You got us in a fine mess you dizzy witch.

Tizzy, Lizzy and Dizzy
Tizzy, Lizzy and Dizzy introduced themselves to Andrella and Barbella.
Welcome to Venice! We are sorry for the spell that summoned you here.
Are you the prestigious Andrella the very powerful good witch of Ozone?

Andrella
Yes I am.

Barbella
Barbella clicking sapphire slippers.
saying in same time they are talking to the Andrella. Optional singing Over the Rainbow.
There is no place like home. There is no place like home. *Again and again till Andrella stops her.*

Tizzy
Can you get us back to London, back to our play Macbeth?

Andrella
I will sure try.
She says , Hickory dickory, reverse the clock, the house moved in a funnel cloud
and moved the clock,
May the witches of Macbeth re appear in their play.
There was a white pouf of smoke but nothing.

Lizzy
That is nice if your out in the open and want to make smoke signals.

Andrella
It seams that Dizzy's spell has us trapped here until she figures out how to reverse her spell.
Barbella that is the wrong spell for getting home, you don't have your ruby slippers on. We are not in OZ ether; Kansas too

Lizzy
We have to find a caldron big enough for our spells to get us home again. There must be one in
Venice.

Andrella
Gets all the witches to huddle with Andrella whispering
You see that handkerchief that is on Othello, It is a enchanted handkerchief that I sense that the holder of it if they are ugly will instantly become more beautiful and with the most impressive charms that a mortal could not do. We have to distract the guards and swipe the handkerchief if off the body. Tizzy and Lizzy you flirt with the guard on the right
Barbella and Dizzy on the left. You meet me down the street, I will run and get the handkerchief off the body
You ready…Go

Lizzy and Tizzy
Flirt with the guard on right getting him to turn away from the corpse.
Hey handsome attracting attention blowing a kiss.

Barbella and Dizzy
Flirt with the guard on left getting him to face left
Hello how about a night on the town blowing a kiss.
The four witches flirt with the guards as they get distracted. Andrella swipes the handkerchief off the body of Othello and runs down the street as fast as she can. Other side of stage.

Andrella
Out of breath, they all run down the same street Andrella did.
This handkerchief only works on ugly people you want to try it see which witch it works on. They all try it, It works on Lizzy.

Lizzy
I am beautiful again, Oh thank you Andrella you are true friends.

Tizzy
We have to find a caldron we will see you both around.

Barbella
We would be much better if we stayed together.

Lizzy:
Oh OK you can hang around with us then.
They all leave the stage.

Crystal
enters stage sees her son hung feet first, breaks out in tears.
Crying
Son… I warned you about being over confident when you have that handkerchief.
Someone has taken his handkerchief. *Looking around*
Holding son. I knew this would happen when you married Desdemona.
Runs off

DESDEMONA
Comes on stage to see Othello hanging in square. As she sees Othello. astonished
OH GOD…My husband is a fraud. He looks so ugly how could this happen___
I know … magic that is my only expiation. My father kept me from making this huge mistake.
My sorrow should be tears of happiness.
Barbantio walks slowly on stage.

DESDEMONA

Father you have shown me who Othello really is. I shall never run from you again, and will ask
your blessing from now on, if I should get married. From now on no wedding unless you can give
me away in the Venice cathedral

Barbantio:
Kisses DESDEMONA
Come my daughter lets go home. A cathedral wedding it is, to a most respectable husband to be.
If I am not available it will still be a wedding in the cathedral.
Holding each other they walk off stage.

Scene three and four.

Characters:
>   Duke of Venice *(no gender bias this can be a mature woman: IE Duchess if Venice)*
>   Duke's Secretary
>   Sheriff of Venice
>   Barbantio
>   Iago
>   Rodegro
>   Cassio
>   DESDEMONA
>   Messenger from Cyprus
>   Ruth the Ruthless Pirate
>   Mr Christanson *Cassio's first mate*
>   Second mate
>   Pirate crewman
>   Casanova

Duke of Venice
(Wakes up to discover the corpse of Othello hanging in the City square.)
Discovers the note on corpse from the attempt to resist arrest from Barbantio; angry)
Sheriff get that corpse down from the city square. Arrange the corpse of Othello to be transported
back to Barcelona. Tell your deputy I want to see Barbantio for what happen last night; for the
conflict with Othello.

Duke of Venice

to secretary

Please send this message to General Iago I wish to have him here before me.

Messenger from Cyprus:

Runs in , with message to the Duke from Cyprus.

Sir the Moors have withdrawn from the Isle of Cyprus they went home to Barcelona.
The Turks have Cyprus under siege. Brutus the Terminator can hold out four weeks at best.
Capture the Colossus Cannon and they can hold out for much more time.
The Colossus cannon was the ultimate weapon of the time like the atom bomb is today.

Duke of Venice:

(to secretary.)

I just hope we have time enough to get our defenses up.

Barbantio:

enters seine to see Duke of Venice

Sire if this is about last night, Othello was offered to surrender and refused to be placed under arrest.

Duke of Venice:

Your action was justified; only the death of the Moor Othello creates a problem for us.
The Moors have become neutral due to the death of the General Othello, the alliance is terminated. The Turks have Cypress under siege. We have four weeks at best to get our defenses up for the eventual invasion of the Turks.

Brabaintio

(Kneeling)

Sir I offer my services as a knight and proven protector of Venice. I will do what is necessary to defend our great city and draft every male over the age of 16 and pick up taxes to support our defensive force.

Duke of Venice:

(Barbantio kneels before the Duke)

Very well I re knight you in the Byzantine army and commander of the militia of Venice. You have the authority to do what is necessary for the commissioning of engineers of defense of the City of Venice.

Barbantio

I will perform my duty with speed and excellence Sire.
(Gets up and leaves the scene)

Iago

Sire you were looking for me

Duke of Venice

Iago, the Turks have Cyprus under siege and the treasure of the Minion is in danger of falling into the Turks hands. We must find the treasure on Cyprus before the Turks. We must capture the Colossus Cannon and use it for defense of our walls Do you have someone to send to take care of this task. There are reports of pirates in the area, If we can get help from them I am willing to grant them amnesty for the crimes against Venice. Here is a map it is only one half of the treasure map. I also want you to command the defense of Venice.

Iago

Cassio is the man for the job with his naval experience he will perform the task. He also has experience with dealing with pirates.
I will summon him and he will set sail immediately. I also will appoint Rodegro commander of all the calvery.   We need that gold for our Catapracts for the armor and horses. Where is the other half of the map?

Duke of Venice

It was stolen by unsavory pirates. Cassio has get the other half of the map from the pirates and find the gold.

Iago

I will acquire some Clydesdales to Cassio so they can move the Colossus cannon. I will recruit the reserve champion swordsmen for the reserve in case of a breach of our walls.

Duke of Venice

Barbantio will be recruiting the militia for the walls and keeps and construction of the defenses of the city.

Cassio

Good morning Iago do you have orders for me today.

Iago

Cassio you are to take your ten ships to the island of Cyprus find the gold that is hidden in the catacombs of the island. We need that gold for the armor for are Catapracts.   You also to take two war horses to the island and capture the famed Colossus Cannon from a garrison of Janessarys that is guarding them. If you should have contact with pirates; you may run into the one that has the other half of the Map. If the pirates help, you can offer amnesty for service to Venice.

Cassio

I am off to my fire ship may anyone that gets in our way, will be roasted like marshmallows.

Scene Four.

(Ruth the Ruthless Pirate is encountered) Casting; she must have strong melee, horseman skills, and be
able to swim well and buxom as well.
Casanova the parrot is computer animation
Stage or set is set up like a ship with the helm.) Music in background Richard Wagner's Flying Dutch
man. The Epic of Iago's Victory starts first scenes of a Greek fire against tall ships that was still in use by
the Byzantine in the 14ᵗʰ century. It looks like spewing Napalm on fire. It was very effective disabling a
tall ship.

Cassio
Mr Christanson! (*Laud*) make sure we are primed to make maximum blast of fire to anyone that
tries to stop us. *While at helm*

Mr Christanson
Yes Sir

Cassio
It is a fine day to be on the water not a cloud in the sky. We are a head of our main fleet, to try to
lure some pirates.

Mr Christanson
If they are near our sole ship will be a attraction to the pirates, We do not want to kill them, just
join us.

Second Mate:
Sir four ships to the port bow!

Cassio
Looks in glass three brigs and frigate, and looks like the flag is…
Pirates. Be prepared for battle, Mr Christanson, full sail, lock all bulge areas in case of breach of
our hull.

Mr Christanson
Bulge areas locked, Sails set full for maximum speed. We are gaining on them fast.

Cassio;
Be prepared to hit their stern with a fire blast. Full sails, spinnaker up!

Second mate:
Three hundred meters and closing fast…
One hundred meters closing fast.

Ruth
Bosom woman, directors discretion ethic background. BBW preferred!
You there be prepared to be boarded and surrender! My elite siege men are aiming at your water line. I will have you swimming before you can say jolly roger.

Cassio
Let them shoot, you have not taken on the likes of a fire ship. The Turks have been trying to sink our fire ships for months.

Ruth
Your out numbered four to one. We will have boarded you before you know it.

Cassio
Bring them on, The likes of hell will be upon you. Men be prepared for battle on our decks, fire on the stern of that frigate.

Ruth
Fire on that ship full broad side. *The four ships fire on the fire ship and do not slow it down. Sounds of broad sides most of the cannons miss the fast fire ship.* Holy Crap that ship is fast. (*They can not turn fast enough) Cannon balls are missing the fast fire ship.*

Cassio
Stay on their stern Mr. Christanson, Full blast of fire to their stern. *Blast of fire on frigate. The frigates decks and cannon holes are engulfed with flame.*
Keep the fire blast up. *The whole pirate ship is in flames.*

Ruth
Most of her men on deck are in flames screaming in pain. They jump in the water for relief.
To the bow of the ship. Holy hell, is upon us. Our helm is on fire. That fire ship is like one big blow torch. Joan of Ark never had it this bad. (*Fanning butt)*

Pirate crewman
To Ruth
Eyer Mam the whole ship will blow, we must surrender! One more blast of that fire ship will be the end of us!

Ruth
Put up the surrender flag! *Runs to her quarters that is all in flames to get the other half of the treasure map.* I never seen anything like this! Hell, Abandon ship!
White flag is up.

Cassio
Mr Christanson! Be prepared to take on survivors. Prepare the brig for prisoners.

Mr Christanson
Yes sir.

Second mate;

Take those prisoners to the brig. The captain wants to see Ruth.

Cassio

Mr Christanson! Signal the rest of our fleet to stay close now. I want to see that pirate captain in
my quarters
Walks to his quarters.

Mr Christanson

Yes sir. I will have her bound before you
In quarters

Cassio

Cassio *in quarters with Ruth*
What is your name?

Ruth

My name is Ruth notoriously named Ruth the Ruthless. What is your name

Cassio

I am Cassio.
Such a beautiful woman as your self how did you end up a pirate. Flirting
I will remove the ropes if you cooperate with me, gently in her ear.

Ruth

My father was a pirate, so I followed the footsteps of my father. We have been hunted by every
navy in Europe. You made fireball of my fathers ship that was handed down to me.

Cassio

I can offer you amnesty from Venice for helping us. You will have a country to live in.

Ruth

You get these ropes off me and I will think about it.
Cassio *Removes ropes*
(Pulls dagger out of her boot and tries to stab Cassio).
Cassio (stops dagger stabbing and attempts to kiss Ruth)
Bites Cassio's lip. Makes it bleed. Slaps Cassio
You try that again, you will get more than a bloody lip.

Cassio

(takes handkerchief to lip)
You have a choice ether be friends with me, or you end up in the brig, with the rest of your crew,
and be abused much more than by myself. Your welcome to sleep in that chair.

Ruth

We can work on being friends slowly, No slam bam thank you mam. *(Pushing Cassio away)*

Cassio

I have no choice to have you sleep in my quarters till we get to Cyprus.
You have something I want, and I have something you want.

Ruth

Sounds intriguing. What is the offer. I really do not like the Turks they sank one of my ships. So
our alliance has very positive possibilities.

Cassio

I offer you half the gold from the treasure of the Minions and live in Venice. Help me with your
corsairs capture the Colossus Cannon. Blow up the Turkish weapons cache.
I need your half of the treasure map.

Ruth

What if I don't? What happens to my crews on my three ships that were in not your grasp of your
fire ship. I will have enough gold to buy a ship of the line. I must have the fire capability of your
ship. I am very impressed the swift damage it does to tall ships.

Cassio

You will hang for piracy under Byzantine and Venice law; your crewmen as well.

Ruth

It sounds like I do not have much choice in the matter or death. I accept your proposal from such
a handsome man. It sounds we have my kind of mission ahead.

Cassio

From such a beautiful lady as yourself we will make a great team in our mission. *Bowing.* Your
welcome to sleep here in my quarters till we get to Cyprus. The treasure is from the ancient
civilization Minion. We have to search the catacombs
and destroy the Turkish weapon cashes. There are rumors that there are deadly booby traps in
those catacombs to get the gold. That is the reason all these centuries no one has found the gold
or died trying.

Ruth

Pushes Cassio on the bed
You go to bed, I will take a bath. I have not seen a bathtub in weeks.

Seine Five:

Directors discretion, details of the sea battle with the Turks.
Computer animation is advised.
(Next morning aboard ship)

Second Mate
Six ships Starboard Bow
yelling on ships rigging

Cassio
Gets Looking glass
Three frigates and three transports looks like. They are Turkish we must sink them they can be a problem later. Iago ordered we are to sink all the transports we can find. With our fire ships we have them out numbered.
Ruth are you with me on this fight?

Ruth
I sure am; we have to make sure they do not make problems for us. Best to get them out of the way.

Cassio
Ruth it be best to signal your brigs to unload their corsairs on the four fire ships and go aboard the DESDEMONA. Have your brigs accompany our two cannon ships in that south cove on Cypress.
Mr Christanson! Signal our cannon ships to go in the south cove.
Signal four fire ships to attack the transports and pick up Ruth to command the ships.
Ruth I trust you would love to get some revenge on the Turks.

Ruth
Will do, death to the Turks! We will make them go down as one big fireball. It be a pleasure to experience a command a fast fire ship. *Ruth transfers to the DESDEMONA by row boat.*

Cassio
Mr Christanson! Full sail up with our spinnaker. Get ready to fire blast them in the stern of those three Turkish Frigates.
Sound of Turkish Cannons.

Mr Christanson
They are firing on us Sir.
Fire over shoots the speeding ship toward the frigates.

Ruth
Gets aboard the DESDEMONA
Are you my first mate!

Mr Romero
Yes mam I am Mr Romero, the captain signaled you your a great sea captain. What orders to you have for me.

Ruth
Mr Romero, Set sail full speed toward those Turkish transports! Get ready for a fire blast were going to have some fireworks!

Mr Romero

Yes mam we are closing fast.

Turkish cannons fire on the Flying Dragon over shoots the ship. This is where the battle has fire spewing at the Turkish fleet everywhere.

Cassio

Mr Christanson! Stay away their broad side full right rudder into their stern.

Mr Christanson

Closing fast sir. Yes sir aiming at their stern.

Second mate:

Four Hundred meters sir… *Turkish Cannon fire over shoots the ships.*

Three hundred meters

Closing with fast within fire range.

Mr Romero

Aboard the DESDEMONA

mam within four hundred meters.

Cannon fire hits ship

Make sure Ballast are secured!

Ruth

Get ready to fire blast those transports.

Mr Romero

One cannon breached our outer hull no speed effect.

Four hundred meters.

Show the Turks giving orders and firing

Cassio

Mr Christanson

Signal the closest ships to Ruth's ships to cover her. All four of our fire ships should be about to fire upon them.

Second mate:

Flying Dragon

One hundred meters within firing range

Flying Dragon fires upon the Turkish frigate with devastating results

Mr Christanson

The helm is one big fire ball sir.

Cassio

Keep firing on them so they can not shoot at us.

Mr Christanson

Eye Sir.

Aboard the Desdemona

Mr Romero

Fire on that transport

Ruth

Mr Romero! Send them to hell! … My daddy would love to see them in one big fire ball. *Fist showing* That's what you get for sinking my daddy's ship! One down two more to go
The DESDEMONA fires on the Turkish ship 100 meters away and it blows up in one big fireball.
One of the other fire ships attack the Turkish transport and a lot of Janessarys jump ship

Cassio

Mr Christanson! Maintain fire to make those cannons feel like ovens.

Mr Christanson!

Yes sir

Second mate

Points they are abandoning ship.
They are abandoning ship

Cassio

Signal our other ships to maintain our attack. *The other three are totally engulfing the Turkish tall ships in flames the Turkish crews are abandoning ship. One of the Turkish ships in a massive explosion of the magazine the ship breaks in two. Greek fire looks like they have Napalm on fire spewing at the Tall ship*

Ruth

Take survivors and put them in the brig.

Mr Romero

Eye Mam.

Cassio

Take on survivors I want to see their captain.

Mr Christanson.

Eye sir.

Cassio

Mr Christanson Notify Ruth we are having a celebration party over the Turks. Better yet just put the captain in the brig.

Mr Christanson

Eye sir.
On the island of Cypress ships in the distance at cove.
Music starts; What do you do with a drunken sailor;
crew breaks open captured Irish whisky all drinking and singing
Crew breaks out in song to Irish song What do you do with a Drunken sailor

Roy the Corsair
Joins the crew Singing

Edward the Corsair
Joins crew singing

John the Corsair
Joins crew singing.

Seine Six

Everyone is camped on the Island of Cypress

Cassio
to Ruth shaking hands
I am very impressed with your seaman ship, *Bows* I sent a message to the Duke
and you have a home Venice. You have been pardoned from the act of Piracy.
Sound of Timpani drums in the distance

Ruth
What about my ship you fire balled. Listen! Wonder why those drums are coming from.
Cassio
$50,000 for you ship is that a fair price? I have herd rumors that there are still remnants of the
Minion civilization on this Island.
Cannon fire in the distance

Ruth
Yes that is a fair price we can settle up when we find the gold.
The Turks must be shelling the fortress.

Cassio
We will first find out were those drums are coming from.

Ruth
Yes, I agree.
From the edge of the encampment

Casanova the Parrot
Rack, Attack.

Ruth
Look a parrot, I'd love to have him

Casanova the Parrot

Rack, wolf whistle heh toots how about you and me..
Rack, How about a kiss and a hug toots.
Rack…Ready Go
Rack… Four ships on the port bow
Rack, Attack!

Ruth

He is about as fresh as you Cassio.

Cassio

I guess every pirate needs
a parrot. Quick get something to eat.
Ruth finds something to eat for Casanova
puts her hand out. Casanova lands on it.

Ruth

That was easy, wonder who had him that knows how to talk
Now I have a parrot.
I lost mine when the Turks sank my one of my ships.

Cassio

I can just see you on the castle wall with the Colossus cannon directing fire on the Turkish invasion force, with the parrot on your shoulder. What are you going to name the parrot?

Ruth

I'll name him Casanova

Cassio

That is a most fitting name.
Lets break camp for where those drums are coming from.

Ruth

I wonder why they are drumming so much. Yes. Good Idea Cassio.
Everyone leaves the stage or area. Ruth and Cassio come back on stage.
Ruth and Cassio find where the drums are coming from.
Cassio and Ruth find the Minion
encampment. Behind some bushes.

Ruth

Look! They are having a ceremony some lady is in the cage.

Cassio

I wonder why.
Both Ruth and Cassio are discovered by remnants of the Minion Civilization warriors several compound
bows are making them walk into the native camp. Casanova fly's away.

Cassio

Look the cave entrance to the gold.

The Minion ceremony is right in front of the entrance to the Minion gold catacomb.
The Minions take Cassio and Ruth and put them in a cage

Ruth

What a fine mess you got us into.
I have no choice now to not be close to you.

Cassio

I hope our men come looking for us.
*Ruth gets more food for Casanova
and Casanova fly's off.*

Cassio

To lady in other cage
Do you understand us.

Lady in Cage

Classy lady dressed very well
Yes I do, What made you come here the Minion's are barbaric?

Ruth

We are Looking for the Minion gold.

Lady in Cage

Well you found the entrance to the gold. That Minion King made a pass at me
he is mad me because he thinks I am a snob.

Cassio

I wonder why we are in cages too..

Lady in Cage

He must be mad at you too.

Ruth

Well Cassio this is our first hazard to get in that cave to get the gold.
Casanova get help!

Cassio

Yes that is very true. Wonder if Casanova can distract the Minions, its almost night fall.

Ruth

My corsairs attack best at night.

Cassio

I hope they do soon .
Casanova fly's off to

73

Near corsair camp.
Near camp

Casanova
Rack, Attack
Rack, Attack
Casanova fly's off back to Minion camp

Ed the Corsair
Ruth must be in trouble, lets go men that's her parrot.
All the corsairs follow Casanova, he stops frequently.
At Minion camp they quietly attack the guards and kill them knifing them or killing them with swords.
At edge of Minion camp they see Cassio and Ruth in a cage. Behind some bushes.
Casanova goes to other side of Minion Camp.

Casanova
Rack, Ready Go
Rack, Ready Go
All the Minions go to other side of camp and follow Casanova pointing at him.
With crossbows the Corsairs attack guards near the cages killing them and opening cage were Cassio and
Ruth are in.
They untie the ropes they are bound with.
Cassio and Ruth escape cages.
Ruth hugs Ed.
Minions discover they have escaped and fire compound bows. Just missing Ruth and Cassio.
The second round of arrows hits Cassio in the arm.

Lady in cage
What about me!
Cassio
Not now lady**!**
To the edge of the cave.
I hope some of my men come. Quick get in the entrance
so those raining arrows don't hit us.
They all run to the edge of the cave behind a rock. Arrows are raining down on them from above. They
hit two corsairs. Then they run into the entrance of cave.
Sound of Crossbow arrows hitting the Minions from other side of the camp.

Mr Christanson
Attack those bow men
Battle takes place with Cassio's crossbowmen and Minion's.
They run away.

Mr Christanson
Are you OK sir I see you are wounded.
I brought the war horses figured you will need them.

I did not hear the drums and thought something is wrong.

Cassio

Your a good man Mr Christanson.
I am ok, we still have to find the gold.
Guard the entrance to the cave while we explore for the gold.

Mr Christanson

Eye Sir

Ruth

To corsairs
Help them guard the entrance to the cave
Casanova flies back to Ruth.

Casanova

Rack, Ready go

Cassio

Best we find out what is in there

Ruth

Casanova fly
Directs Casanova to fly into cave
Casanova sets off giant rolling pin that is rolling out of the catacomb and loses a feather.
flying back out the men and Ruth a mad rush out of the entrance to get out of the way
most of entrance is blocked. Director discretion on rolling pin and huge rock that blocks the entrance.
Starts the scene with a bang though
Ruth directs Casanova to fly into cave again.

Ruth

Fly Casanova
Casanova flies into the cave again
he sets off another booby trap.
A big stone round rock comes rolling out of catacomb
blocks the entrance entirely.
It cracks the rolling pin almost in half.
Casanova manages to fly back to Ruth
Cassio directs men *to take one of the Clydesdale horses and get gear and powder for pulling that rolling pin out of the way.*

Cassio

Mr Christanson, Get the pulling gear for the colossus cannon and all the ropes you can to get that rolling pin out of the way. Also get some powder from the captured supplies and bring it here we may have to blow it out of the way.
Casanova is a life saver Ruth.

Mr Chiristanson

Eye Sir

Ruth

You have that right. We be all squished if it was not for him.

How is your arm Cassio?

Cassio

It stings and is painful.

Actually that last rolling rock may have helped us get that rolling pin out of the way.

Ruth

Ruth pulls Cassio to safety.

Lets hope so, Lie down *gets Cassio to lie down to get arrow out of his shoulder.*

Nurses Cassio and gets some whisky to disaffect wound.

Finds something to stop the bleeding and

Caresses Cassio's Hair.

Is that better?

Cassio

That whisky stings, Yes much better.

Ruth

Then I must attend to the wounds of my men.

Mr Christanson

Rushing back on horse to get the ropes and gear.

I will get the ropes and gear for the gold

All exit stage

Act II
Seine I

The Minion catacombs

Ed the Corsair

(to Ruth)

Charges set, to blow those rocks to pieces that block the entrance of the catacombs

Ruth

Lets hope this works. Take cover

They all take cover

Sound of a huge exposition, the rocks are just small rocks that can be moved.

Cassio

I hope the Turks did not hear that explosion. Mr Christanson
get the men to clear that entrance get all our men to help.

Ruth

We better he ready if they show up station the men on guard. Cassio what do you want to do with
that lady in the cage think we should rescue her?

Cassio *(to Ruth)*

You talk to her, if she is snobby keep her there.

Ruth

OK. *Ruth goes over to cage to talk to her*
To lady
So what did the king did not like about, what you said to him.

Lady in cage

Get me out of here you useless tramp.

Ruth

Be careful what you call useless, your the one in the cage.
I think I will wait till we are done in the catacombs to deal with you.

Lady in the cage

You low life, poor excuse for a woman.
You scum bag, useless piece of trash!

Ruth

laughs. It is confirmed you are a snob. With a foul mouth as well.
I see there is a good reason your in that cage.
I will see you when we are done in the catacombs.

Lady in cage

I am a professional actress and a dancer I do not deserve this kind of treatment.

Ruth

Its confirmed, a elitist as well

Cassio

It is looking like we have at least a hole to get into the catacombs again
we better make it bigger in case our men and horses have to enter.

Ruth

(goes over to Cassio ,orders corsairs to help)
Help Cassio's men
Cassio the Minion king put that lady in the cage for a GOOD reason.

Cassio

Well we will have to deal with her later; best not have to put up with her when we are in there.

Ruth

We better bring some men in with us never know what is in there.

Cassio

As long as we don't end up squished by rocks.

Have several cross bow men come in with us.

Both Ruth and Cassio go in the catacomb together light torches to see.

All of a sudden a ball of fire comes toward them and a loud noise.

Ruth

(all of them singed by fireball)

Look its a giant fire spider. Kill it!

All men swarm the spider to kill it

Cassio

Well that's over lets be very careful everyone Ruth stay close to me.

Ruth

Yes! Cassio my pet.

Another giant spider comes toward them.

This one is clear as glass.

Two Zombies appear and come toward them.

Cassio

Kill it, and get the Zombies.

They swarm the spider and kill it. The Zombies disappear.

Ruth

That was something to write about! Glass dread spiders.

I have herd of them; we have seen one first hand.

They go deeper into the catacomb and they hear the sound of water rushing.

From the side of the cave a giant rock that is in form of a man attacks them.

Cassio

Kill it everyone. *Their swords clank on the feldspar rock giant and kills one of the men, they finally kill it. They damage their weapons.*

Ruth

I hope we do not encounter many more of those.

Cassio

We better look out for the rocks too in this place.

Ruth

Listen, That sounds like a underground river.

They go deeper into the catacomb to a opening that a underground river is blocking their path. Signs of a old bridge is there but is not serviceable.

Cassio

Looks like that bridge has seen its days. We have to build another solid one if we are going to get the gold out. Better replace our weapons in case another giant rock attacks us. Mr Christanson order the men to get as much wood as they can for building a bridge across that river. We better make a pontoon bridge so it can carry a lot of weight. We can use some life boats from the Turkish ships we sunk.

Ruth

Looks like we have a lot of work to be done. A lot of major moving of supplies those Clydesdale horses will be use a lot.

Cassio

The correct term for it is we have to call the engineers in to make the bridge.
The catacombs is big enough for a horse being in here not much more though.

Ruth

What's a engineer?

Cassio

They are the builders of civilizations Ruth.
Guess your education was mostly on ship.
The time spent will be worth it

Ruth

My daddy taught me is get the gold and have plenty to eat.
How to defend myself in battle if attacked. Keep away from strangers and only trust another pirate with caution.
Cassio don't we have to be back in Venice at a certain time?

Cassio

Well looks like we will have our share of battles in here. Your daddy's teaching will serve you well. The duke rather me be late, and with the gold, than without it.

Ruth

My men are good at robing and stealing never asked them to help build a bridge.

Cassio

There is all ways a first time we can use their help.

Ruth

Well there better be a good share of gold for us

Cassio

I do not think the Minions would take the time to set up those booby traps we all ready
encountered if it was not worth it to protect.

Ruth

We have to get some men on the other side to set up the foundation for the pontoon bridge. We
can make a raft to ferry across it will serve us well to building the bridge.

Cassio

Your not a engineer Ruth, but you have a lot of sense to make up for it.
Mr Christanson brings in the horses with a load of wood the men start making a bridge.

Mr Christanson

Building supplies came from the wrecks of the Turkish fleet.
It will be a few days until the bridge is built.

Cassio

We may be building the first underground pontoon bridge in history that is quite accomplishment.
Lets hope there is no sharks in the waters.

Ruth

Singing

Anchors away me boys build that bridge for our gold men is on the other side.
No singing Get the rope for connection to the other side..
Both Cassio's men and Ruth's build the bridge with sounds of hammering.

Cassio

Yes, the foundation to the other side has to be solid.
I just got a idea for those giant rock men ,sledge hammers.

Ruth

Sledge hammers

Cassio

They will crack those things faster than a sword.

Ruth

I am not carrying no heavy sledge hammer.

Cassio

Well have one of your men carry one.

Ruth

Well if you say so guess its worth a try.

Cassio

Its getting late we better make camp outside

Ruth
All this fighting I'm hungry

Cassio
How about some pasta with cheese sauce. And garlic.

Ruth
That sounds good

Cassio
Do you like garlic

Ruth
I love garlic

Cassio
Then we will make a fire and a big pot of pasta for the men. The sauce reeks with garlic.

Ruth
You don't get kisses from me with you smelling like garlic.
They walk outside and make camp
That lady is still in the cage I am going to let her out she has suffered enough.

Cassio
She must be hungry, I will start dinner
Ruth walks to lady in cage

Ruth
I'm back, Your invited for some dinner
She lets her out of the cage

Lady in cage
Thank you this cage is torture.

Ruth
It has been effective, your not a snob to me anymore.

Lady in Cage
Anything to get out of that cage
They both walk to camp, Lady in the cage sits down for dinner.

Ruth
When is that pasta going to be ready.

Cassio
In a few minutes get something to drink.

Ruth

I have some Irish whisky.

Cassio

I want the men sober in the morning.

Ruth

Black berry juice.

Cassio

That is good, Sure is a beautiful night
Ruth hugs Cassio while he is cooking

Ruth

Is the pasta ready?

Cassio

It looks like it is, You want extra garlic on it.

Ruth

No thank you.

Cassio

I am putting some on mine.

Ruth

Well I am not staying close to you your going to smell like garlic for days.
Holding nose

Cassio

Well its better than all the blood sucked out of me; we may encounter Vampires.
The lady in the Cage leaves the camp after she is done eating.
I'm going to bed.
Seine is dark
They wake up in the morning light.

Ruth

To Cassio
Good morning
I guess we have to wait till that bridge is finished.

Cassio

Just enjoy this beautiful day with you here its makes it all worth while.
Have you seen Casanova?

Ruth

Maybe he flew away.

Casanova flies on Ruth's shoulder

Casanova
RACK heh toots.

Ruth
you stay close to me.

Casanova
RACK Ready Go

Ruth
Maybe you can distract those rock giants.
she feeds him

Casanova
RACK, Attack, Attack

Cassio
Wonder where the Minions went? Have you seen that lady?

Ruth
I never want to see them again the way they treated us. They probably went across the island.
Good riddance.
Oh that lady disappeared after dinner probably to find away off this island..

Cassio
That is where Brutis the Terminator is
I wonder how they are doing.
We better hurry and get our mission done.
I am sure he needs the weapons caches destroyed.

Ruth
I am sure once the bridge is done things will happen quickly.

Cassio
No use sitting around we can destroy some weapons caches while the bridge is being built.

Ruth
Are you crazy we have half our men working on building that bridge

Cassio
I have ten men to spare, Do you have any that can break way.

Ruth
I can ask for volunteers I am sure they rather be blowing something up than building a bridge.

She goes over to her men.
I need men to blow up ammo caches.
Eight men volunteer.

Ruth
Looks like we have 18 to help.
I rather blow them up now, than have them loaded in hand cannons in Venice.

Cassio
We leave camp at nightfall. We will scout for the weapons caches.
It will give Brutis some relief from the siege on them.
Seine changes to them hiding near a Turkish encampment
You see that big box it must be the weapons cache for this encampment.
Looks like it's guarded well.

Ruth
Ed you see those boxes have the men set charges next to them and get back here.
Kill the guards and make it quiet.

Ed the Corsair
Yes Mam

Ruth
Maybe we can have Casanova distract them.
Fly Casanova
Casanova flies over them they start shooting at him.
He perches on the box

Casanova
RACK, Attack, Attack
He flies away the guards scramble after him.
Ruth's corsairs set the charges and head back to Ruth.
A tremendous explosion

Cassio
That bird is the hero tonight.

Ruth
Lets get out of here!
They scramble off

Scene II

Entrance to catacombs
Both Cassio and Ruth are walking in the Catacomb.

Cassio
We should check out the progress of the bridge

Ruth
I hope it is done.

Cassio
I have my sledge hammer ready.
For the feldspar rock Giants

Ruth
I hope we never see another one of those.

Cassio
I have a feeling that we have not seen the last of them.
Oh I sent a message to the Duke recommending you into knighthood.

Ruth
Sounds too masculine to me.

Cassio
I love to see their face when you beat a man when you lift up your visor.

Ruth
I like beating a man in a traditional mans role.
The British do not take too kindly to women that wear pants.
They think they are all witches
Did you hear what happen to Joan of Ark?
I wear pants what is the difference.

Cassio
So if you run into one of those British you can put them in their place.

Ruth
I sure will.
They see Mr Christanson
Cassio gives him a hand shake.

Cassio
Is the bridge done

Mr Christanson
It sure is. It looks weird it is a wonder what you can do with the remnants of sunken ships. It will service us well to get the gold out.

Cassio
Have the men ready to go deeper into the catacomb

Mr Christanson
Yes sir.

Ruth
Ed have the men ready to go with them. Stay close.

Ed
Will do mam.
They walk slowly deeper into the catacomb
Ruth smells something burning.
Stravinsky music The Firebird; directors discretion in background Music. During battle with Fire giants. Dance of the Earth. Suggested.
They go in the catacomb farther

Ruth
LOOK ..FIRE GIANTS!
Three fire giants slowly come toward them
Retreat and Shoot!
all the men retreat and shoot at the Fire giants,
They kill one of them.

Cassio
Retreat men then shoot your crossbows. It seams to be working.
Stay close Ruth.
They kill another fire giant

Ruth
I will my pet!
They retreat then shoot at the last one.
Ruth hugs and kisses Cassio. The relationship of the two of them is getting to be "Special".
If Casanova flew over them would be a firebird than a parrot with those coming at us. *Casanova is on Ruth's Shoulder.*

Casanova
Rack. Attack, Attack

86

Cassio

Well best we make some progress to our goal. It is a good thing they did not get to the bridge it be
burned for sure.
They all walk slowly deeper into the catacomb.
*Another rock giant from the wall attacks them. With the grunts from the feldspar rock giant a fire flash
hits one of the men.*
Cassio hits him with the sedge hammer cracks it in pieces.
That's something, Geology that moves. My idea works does wonders on those things.

Ruth

Such prowess impresses me. Ed take one of the sledge hammers and help Cassio.

Ed the Corsair.

Eye mam Will do!
They take the right catacomb when they come upon it

Ruth

I hope this is the right way.

Cassio

If not we try the other one no problem.

Ruth

That is if we do not end up dead in the process.

Cassio

I think we have seen the worst of this place.

Ruth

We can end up squished from one of those rolling rock booby traps.

Cassio

Have Casanova fly ahead of us to scout for us.

Ruth

Fly Casanova

Casanova

RACK, Right toots.
Casanova fly's a head and touches off a ax Gauntlet. They are swinging back and forth.

Cassio

He bows to Ruth, Your knights training awaits.
Looks at Casanova.
I love that bird! *With blowing a kiss.*

Ruth
We would end up sliced and diced if it were not for him.
Go in between the axes when they are swinging.

Cassio
Move fast when its clear! Some you may have to duck to the floor.
They all try to avoid the swinging axes. One of the crossbowmen gets killed by one of the swinging axes.
Move fast men when its clear do not hesitate.
That is what keeps you alive in this gauntlet.
This is a sign we are going in the right direction.

Mr Christanson
With this gauntlet we have to carry the gold out there must be a way to deactivate it so our horses
can come in. They be sliced to pieces if they tried to come in.
I will stay behind. They have pendulums that make these work if I can disable them they be stuck
in one position.
They all get past the gauntlet

Cassio
Make it so number one. We may have to carry the gold out past the gauntlet.

Ruth
Lets get to it first before we plan anything.
They proceed further and come in contact with more giant fire spiders two men are hit by a fire blast.
They all swarm around them to kill them.

Cassio
Are you taking notes Ruth, this place is something to write about.

Ruth
Rather worry about drowning, this place gives me the creeps.
LOOK! THAT LIGHT!
They proceed down the catacomb and see a bright light at the end of the tunnel.

Cassio
I wonder what is making that light in this dark place.
(They all go to the light at the end of the tunnel.
They get to a room with three tons of gold.
Guarding it is twelve vampires.)
The walls are lit up. the rocks put off a natural light.

Ruth
Quick Cassio blow at them!
This room its beautiful the rocks just light up this room no torches.
One of the Vampires

Vampire

I smell garlic lets get out of here!

All the Vampires

GARLIC!

(The twelve vampires smell Cassio from the garlic. They turn into bats and fly away. Up a to a opening to the surface.)

Ruth

Giggles, Cassio I will never complain about you eating garlic again! You saved us. *The men shake Cassio's hand. But they do smell the garlic on him and hold their nose.*
The death of Ed is to signify greed sometimes ends up in death.
It not worth their life for anything.

Ed the Corsair

LOOK that Idol I must have it!
ED runs to get his hands on the Idol.
And picks it up.

Casio and Ruth

Ed NO don't touch it!
Sound of trap door-
All of a sudden the booby trap, trap door opens up.
He falls into a bottomless pit that we hear him saying help.
He falls to his death with the idol in hand.

ED The Corsair

Heeeeelp!

Ruth

In tears crying hugging Cassio-- Cassio I lost my best man!
Cassio tries to comfort Ruth.

Cassio

You know the risks there were coming in here dear. (*And kisses her.*)
(Pauses with silence embracing Ruth)
Everyone do not touch anything that would be religious idols the Minions took them very seriously. As you just saw greed sometimes ends up in death.
There is another one on the wall that they consider the goddess of fertility, DO NOT TOUCH IT.
He points at it.
Everyone poke with a long stick first before you lift any gold up.
You see the results of a lot of shrewd trading. The Minions had no resources to trade with, but shear merchant genius.

Ruth

I never seen so much gold.

Cassio

We can armor a fifteen hundred Catapracts with this gold. Ruth you can have a super fire ship if you want it.

Tell Mr. Christanson to get the rest of the men to carry out this gold.

Ruth

To second mate- Help Cassio's men to get this gold out.

What are Catapracts? (*Looking at him, flirting).* I might not want that ship.

Cassio

A Cataract were used by the Romans and our army that were the ultimate heavy calvery. They have to use huge horses we have two of them; to carry the weight of the armor that they carry. The Turkish hand canons shot will bounce off the armor its that good.

1500 Catapracts can cut down and run over a lot of Janssarys in defense of Venice.

Ruth

I like to see that!

Cassio

I think with you manning the Colossus Cannon you will have a excellent view of the battle if there is one. Lets hurry and get this gold out.

Casanova

RACK, Ready Go.

Ruth

UHH (the weight of the gold) *She picks up all the gold she can, and carry's it out.*

Goody, I like blowing up weapons caches. Are we doing that next?

One of Cassio's men deliver message from Mr Christanson

Cassio

Great! the Gauntlet is disabled. We can get the horses and cart into this room and get this gold out faster.

I wonder what kind of rock that makes the light. In this room sure is pretty.

YES Ruth we will have Brutus smiling tomorrow night.

Ruth

Who cares about the stupid rock, we got what we came for! Lets get this gold to the ships. Love to see Turks scurry, trying to get at Casanova, while their weapons caches blow up.

Casanova

Rack, Right toots

Cassio

Best of all the first phase of our mission is ACOPLISHED we must celebrate!
Ruth tonight we break out the whisky.

Ruth

Well that sounds good, your not having any, I have other plans for US.*(Flirting)*

Seine III

Turkish Weapons Cache mission
Men sing "What do you do with a drunken Sailor"
in camp. Dancing too. Directors discretion.

Ruth

In Tent in bed with Cassio
Lying in bed with Cassio in the morning. Whispering in Cassio's ear.
Was it good last night? You fell a sleep before I could ask you.

Cassio

Yes dear I could take a life time of that,

Ruth

I may take you up on that the way things are going.
It was good for me too.
The way you arbitrated that giant feldspar rock person.
Such a turn on for me. Such prowess.
Fingers caressing threw Cassio's hair.

Cassio

We should get to the weapons cashes at night fall.

Ruth

I love things that go Boom in the night.

Casanova

RACK, Ready Go

Cassio

Lets break camp and hike across the island to the weapons caches.
We should have all the gold in the ships too before we take off.

Ruth

Gets out of bed
I rather sail for there. I hate hiking all that way.

91

I will make sure we have plenty of powder for our task at hand.
Gets out of the tent tells second mate.
Gather plenty of powder for tonight. Load it in with a horse and the cart for going across the island.

Second mate
Right will do.

Ruth
Cassio it is a beautiful morning not a cloud in the sky. Last thing we want is wet powder.

Cassio
Mr Christanson stay here and get all that gold. Do not touch the idols though. Anyone that touches them it is certain death.

Mr Christanson
It should not be more than three loads, I will have the ships loaded by tonight..

Cassio
Make sure the gold is not in just one ship and make sure its a fire ship. They have two hulls and less likely to sink.

Ruth
Come on Cassio we better get going.

Casanova
RACK. Ready Go
RACK. Right toots

Cassio
OK I am coming.
They are hiking

Ruth
Oh look there is a Deer. I never seen one.

Cassio
How do you know that is a deer? It could be a elk or moose.

Ruth
Not big enough for a elk or moose.
Still hiking.
Cassio did you ever think of settling down and having a family?

Cassio
I have been at sea most of my life like you.

Ruth
I always wondered how it be like with a family instead of being at sea.
A bed for one is no fun. Last night was special for me.

Cassio
I always wondered how it be like. It was special for me too.

Ruth
We can have lots of little nasty pirates.

Cassio
Chuckles, Yeh right. It sounds good though, we have to first live threw this.

Ruth
I have a feeling it has been destiny that how we met. Nothing like that will happen I will make sure of it.

Cassio
What makes you so sure nothing will happen.

Casanova
RACK, Right Toots

Ruth
It be you me and Casanova, Get married it a grand church.

Cassio
We are getting a little ahead of ourselves. It does sound good though.
We do have some possible serious combat to go threw.

Ruth
The thought though it be so grand.
The sound of Jannesary fire and cannons in the distance.

Cassio
We must be getting close to the battle the weapons caches must not be far off.

Ruth
You make a romantic event fizzle out with your military matters.

Cassio
We must think of the mission we have to accomplish. I am willing to make the commitment that is the best I can do for now.
Still hiking

Ruth
Look this looks like a good place to camp till night fall.

Cassio

No fires give that message too all our men get the powder ready we are making things go boom tonight.

Ruth

The way you said that Cassio, Going "Boom in the night"
I love it. *Hugs Cassio*
Nightfall all the stars out clear night

Ruth

Look Cassio the stars, with tonight's fireworks it going to be so grand.

Cassio

Yes it is, one of the men scouting found four weapons caches

Ruth

Well lets get out of here, You ready Casanova?

Casanova

RACK, Ready GO
RACK, Attack, Attack

Cassio

The poor Turks they have not seen Casanova.

Ruth

Very soon they will, It was a great diversion. With the Minions
Hiding behind some bushes.

Cassio

There are the four weapons caches that our scout found.

Ruth

Fly Casanova!
Casanova fly's to the weapons cache and perches himself on one of them.

Casanova

RACK, ATTACK, ATTACK
RACK, ATTACK ,ATTACK

Casanova fly's to the other side of the encampment, the Turk's follow. Ruth's Corsairs sneak to the weapons cashes and set the charges to the weapons caches. They kill some of the guards with knives. Casanova fly's to another location with the Turks following. Casanova fly's to Brutus's fortification and they shoot the guards. Scene of Brutis on the wall optional.

Cassio

This is too easy. I love that bird. Let get out of here!

There is a tremendous blast that lasts four minutes long that lights the sky.
They stop running for a second to look.

Ruth
LOOK Honey Fireworks.
She gives Cassio a hug and a kiss and they continue running

Cassio
That is a pretty sight. With the stars too.
Break camp to another location. The Turks will be looking for us.
This is were things can get bloody. Have one of our Scouts look for the location for the Colossus
cannon.

Scene IV

(Quest for the Colossus Cannon)

Cassio
Now that we did some major damage to the Turks they are going to be scouting for us.

Ruth
Well we best not avoid contact with them give the order to avoid combat unless its necessary.

Cassio
That may be hard to do with them having the order to shoot on sight.

Ruth
I have had six nations navy's looking for me and here I am, so what, with them wanting to shoot at
me on sight.
The Fireworks last night was sure pretty.

Cassio
Did you notice something there is no Janessary or cannon fire today.
We must have got all their weapons supplies so they can not attack. It is ether that or they are out
looking for us.

Ruth
So don't they have crossbows?

Cassio
The Turkish army is strictly gunpowder units.

Ruth
Well they are down to throwing rocks now. No slingers ether.

Cassio

No slingers ether they quit using them long time ago. Slingers took rocks and with a sling threw
them at the enemy quite effective really.

Ruth

Well they might as well pack up and go home.

Cassio

They still have one weapon that can breach Brutus's fortifications, and we are out to get it. We have
been extremely lucky with very few losses.
Scout approaches Cassio.

Scout

Sir I have seen a big cannon that the wheels do not look big enough to take it away.

Cassio

That's great we are off to the Colossus Cannon location.
They are trying to stay out of sight when they get Hand cannon fire from a Turkish scouting party.

Ruth

Duck for cover.

Cassio

Crossbowmen fire a volley toward them.
A rain of arrows comes down the Janesarys's
kills most of them, the rest run off.

Ruth

Quick lets get out of here before more come.

Cassio

Best to capture the cannon at night. In the mean time we must stay out of sight I thought I saw a
cave on the way here maybe we can hide in there until its time.

Ruth

I rather hide in bushes than go in another catacomb

Cassio

OK the bushes it is.
Here is a good place were we can not be seen.

Ruth

Just like I wanted among all the danger. *She kisses him while they are hiding and lying in the bushes.*
They make love among all the danger.
We get to do this till night fall. *She kisses him again*

Cassio

Why fight it, I hope they do not find our horse for the cannon.

Ruth
Don't worry if we do not have a horse we will steal theirs.
One time we had to steal a horse it got taken back three times, we still got it in the end.

Cassio
Since when did you need a horse.

Ruth
We were pillaging a Moorish outpost and we needed a horse to get to ship.

Cassio
So how many places have you raised and pillaged.

Ruth
She counts on her fingers. Total six, Ed had to rescue me from imprisonment.
We burned the place down. After that I got the name Ruth the Ruthless.

Cassio
After that your reputation went like wild fire,

Ruth
It get harder to stay out of sight after that.
So what about you, my fearless Officer. *(Flirting)*

Cassio
Well I joined the navy at age 16 and been at sea ever since. I got promoted when I took this our
missions after leaving Venice.
The duke knew my reputation for dealing with pirates and was impressed and here I am.
I became a sea captain protecting Byzantine merchant ships. I came in contact with my share of
pirates. Mostly I did service near Constanople. After that I moved to Venice.

Ruth
It is starting to get dark.

Cassio
We can expect a harder time and they will be shooting at anything now.

Ruth
I have had whole towns wanting to shoot me, not much difference.

Casanova
Rack, Ready GO!

Cassio
Time to move out and get that cannon.

They hike to the spot and hide behind some bushes.

Ruth

I count at least a dozen Janessarys guarding that cannon.

Cassio

You want to try our diversion tactic. with Casanova

Ruth

It is worth a try.
FLY Casanova.

Casanova

RACK, Attack, Attack.
Casanova flies and perches on the canon

Casanova

RACK, ATTACK , ATTACK
He flies to the edge or the encampment
The Janessarys just stay at their posts and shoot at him.
Casanova just flies off. He looses feathers.

Cassio

I was afraid of that; order the Crossbowmen a fire rain of arrows on them.
They kill six the first volley. FIRE, .The rest of the Janessarys fire back killing three crossbowmen.

Ruth

Wish my men can help this a range weapon battle.
(The crossbowmen fire again and kill the rest of the Janessarys.)
Quick men with the horse pull that cannon out of their camp before they know its gone. *They rush to the cannon*
(They attach the cannon to a harness and pull the cannon out of camp)
Ruth is on the horse that is pulling the cannon

Cassio

We must not stop until we get to our ships in the cove. Hurry everyone. We are lucky no guards survived that last volley of arrows.
(They make a mad dash for their ships cove, 10 minutes later they hear a bell.)
Some exiting seines can be made with them rushing back to the ships. Ducking branches and the cannon bouncing up and down.

Ruth

They finally realized their cannon was no where to be found.
To the ships! *(everyone is rushing to get back to the ships.)*
The Turks follow the tracks of the cannon chasing after them.

Cassio

I hope Mr Christanson had some of our men set up a defensive position
at the cove. (*He is still rushing to get back to the cove.*)

Ruth

I hope so too.
(*They finally get to the cove*)

Cassio

Mr. Chiristanson is the gold loaded? Prepare for a battle with the Turks following us.

Mr Christanson

Gold is loaded sir, They will wish they never came here. Men prepare for a attack.
(*Cassio's men get into defensive positions ready for battle.*)

Ruth

Hurry men get that canon aboard the DESDEMONA. Set it up to fire at the Turks.
Make way to set sail. *They set up and load the cannon. They kill five Turks with a loud boom of the cannon.*
I love this cannon!
Signal the rest of my ships to follow us.

Second mate

Eye mam

Cassio

Mr Chiristanson take command of the Flying Dragon I will go with Ruth
(*Twenty Turks approach the defensive line are all killed.*)

Mr Christanson

Will do sir*!*
Aboard the Flying Dragon

Mr Christanson

Make way to set sail to Venice**.** Signal the other ships to follow us.

Cassio

Make sure the ships with the gold are close to the other ships in case of a enemy attack.
To Ruth.
Was it worth the risk dear?

Ruth

YES my pet, and a better half too. This was such a adventure, So many things we encountered
along the way.
Cassio picks Ruth up with a very long kiss
Aboard the Flying Dragon

Lady in Cage
To Mr Chiristanson comes out of below decks
Finally off that retched island, where are we going?

Mr Chiristanson
We are going to Venice. How did you get on ship/

Lady in Cage
Are any theaters there or dance halls? I stowed away.

Mr Chiristanson
Yes there are three in fact.

Lady in Cage
Heh your cute. *Kisses Mr Chiristanson. While he is at the helm of the ship*
Holding his arm
Closes with the sight of the fleet setting sail. With a gold Sunrise shimmering on the water. End of first third of Iago's Victory. Defense of the City Venice is next,

Act III
The Defense of the City of Venice

Scene 1

Dukes governors building
Cassio and Ruth are to report to the Duke
In front of building

Cassio
Well this were the city government is Ruth.

Ruth
This is one time I am here not to ransack the place.

Cassio
Chuckles, no your not we are to see the Duke and report our official success of our mission.

Ruth
You know, it does not seam fair you have to give away your half of the gold.
If we got married then you can share my half.

Cassio

We will dear, lets get threw the defense of the city.

Ruth
Well you promise not to leave me. I am in a strange city with a lot of strangers.

Cassio
I promise I will not leave you. The Duke is expecting us.
They both walk into the Dukes government chambers.
Cassio and Ruth Bow

Cassio
Sire I am return from my missions on the Island of Cypress
May I present Ruth that helped us immensely and her parrot Casanova.

Duke of Venice
From my messages from Cypress you really did a job on the Turks.
So well they withdrew from the island and Brutis the Terminator is still with us.
OH by the way your now Admiral Cassio now.
Is this our new KNIGHT or should I say Admiral, Or both.

Cassio
May I present Ruth sir, Both sir
Thank you sir.
Ruth elbows him in the ribs.

Duke of Venice
Ruth kneel before me.
Ruth Kneels
I there fore Christen thee Sir Ruth the Admiral

Ruth
You mean I am the same rank as Cassio.

Duke of Venice
Hesitates and Cassio encourages him by body gesture.
Yes you are.

Ruth
What about my amnesty for me and my men

Duke of Venice
Full pardon just like we promised. I do not know about other countries though.
As long as your in Byzantine territory you have no problem.

Ruth
I request that all my missions are in Byzantine waters.

Cassio is again giving gestures to say yes, to the Duke.

Duke of Venice
hesitates, looks at Cassio
That can be arrange we will do our best.
Now the business at had just how much gold does the government get from your find.

Cassio
One and a half tons of Gold sire minus the cost of Ruth's ship.
Half like we agreed went to Ruth and her men.

Ruth
Forget the ship, Cassio and I have plans for our future together.
Sire I donate 500 pounds of gold for the Catapracts.

Duke of Venice
Such a donation is welcome; it will be used for the Catapracts to defend the city.
I need you both at a meeting with Iago and Rodegro and Barbantio for a strategy meeting for defense of the city. In about one hour.

Cassio and Ruth
Yes sire we will be there
They both exit, and they meet Rodegro.

Cassio
Rodegro how is the training of our Catapracts going?
May I present SIR Ruth the Admiral.
And bows.

Rodegro
I commend you both for your successful missions, I have 1500 fine Catapracts that need their armor. Such a beautiful lady as well.
Ruth bows.

Cassio
We just gave the duke enough gold to armor all your men Rodegro.

Rodegro
We have the best calvery in all of Europe;
with them armored we can cause the Turks a lot of damage. I am in forever in your debt to both of you. I will have the blacksmiths working night and day to get them outfitted.

Ruth
We have the best cannon to cover them as well. It was defiantly life changing..

Cassio

Its almost time for our meeting.
They walk into the meeting where Iago and the Duke are presiding.

Seine III

Plans for defense of the city.
(Peril the Fruit vendor is presented)

Iago

I first like to make a toast our Admirals Cassio and Ruth to their most successful mission.
They all stand and make a toast to Cassio and Ruth.

Iago

Barbantio what is the progress on the city walls and the militia to man them?

Barbantio

We have Six castles under constriction and they are behind walls. Behind the walls in key places
are keeps that are behind the walls for command and control.
We are strongest our south wall that has the most exposure. I found 20 hand Greek fire. We
have two thousand men to man the walls, keeps and castles, I hear we have the famed Colossus
cannon that will be at the south castle that is on a hill.

Cassio

To Ruth whispers to her.
That's were your going to be, and Casanova in the south castle. Watching the whole battle. *Ruth
smiles*

Iago

I have 1500 champion swordsmen in reserve in case the walls are breached. 20 men with the hand
Greek Fire.

Rodegro

I have 1500 men that are trained as Catapracts I just got news that they will be heavily armored for
shot from Jassesarys. We have the most formidable calvery ever assembled. It they land we will hit
and run and ruin their supply line. When they attack our walls we will take out a good portion of
them that are near our walls. We will also neutralize their siege weapons.

Cassio

We have our 8 fast fire ships and our 2 tall ships plus two brigs to intercept the Turkish fleet.
Ruth will be close to shore if they land; she and her men will go to the south castle to man the
Colossus cannon.

Duke of Venice

I am most pleased in the progress of the defenses of our city. I just got a message from Constanople that 6000 Janessarys have broken the siege of the city and boarded ships, and they are heading our way. Cassio and Ruth you may as well saved Constanople too. The loss of their cannon I think that what made them to break off to Venice. The force that they have in siege around Constanople now they can hold out indefinitely. They are more of a nuance to them than anything.

This meeting is adjourned.

They all exit the building

Peril is waiting for Rodegro outside in Venice square.

Iago is there too.

The rest go home

Peril the Fruit Vendor

Rodegro, are you coming to my villa? DESDEMONA Will be there we can invite Iago too for a fun time. We will have pasta a sprits, please come.

Rodegro

Sounds good are you coming Iago.

Iago

I could use a break from training men. Count me in.

at Peril's villa

DESDEMONA is making pasta.

Both Rodegro and Iago look astonished at Desdemona.

Iago

Desdemona you have got bigger.

Rodegro

A lot bigger, from the last time we saw you running out of your house.

Desdemona

Directors discretion this screenplay is BBW friendly

Ever since the death of Othello all I have been doing is eating pasta and sleeping. Stuffing myself with sweets too. Oh wine too.

Iago

You developed a nice butt. More pushin'

Cushin'

They are all at the table eating

Desdemona

Don't you love it, biggest butt in all of Venice.

Turns and shows her butt.

They are all at the table eating

Peril the fruit vendor

Do you like that Rodegro? I can do that too. Get a big butt like hers.

Rodegro

I sense Desdemona is setting a trend in our women Iago *laughing.*

Iago

I like much more to hold than skin and bones. What do you think of Cassio's girl friend Ruth.

Rodegro

She is very beautiful lady.

Iago

The duke knighted her, she can enter in jousting tournaments. She must be quite a swordsman.
Cassio tells me her father taught her well how to fight.
You know she was the most ruthless pirate on the seas.

Peril

Rodegro you want some wine? She kisses Rodegro.

Rodegro

Yes!

Kisses Peril

Desdemona

You know speaking of a jousting tournament. Venice should have a jousting tournament

Iago

Your defiantly a knights daughter. Its not a bad idea. I will suggest it to the Duke; Invite knights
from all over the land.

Desdemona

There is one knight though I dread coming to the tournament.
He has had a crush on me for years.

Peril

Who is that?

Desdemona

He is the Dread Black Knight from Masadonia. I do not know what I would do if he showed up.

Iago

He is a fierce competitor even better than Othello was.
If your the prize I think anyone that got in his way would be killed. We would have to stop the
contest before he did it.
It is sure nice night, Full moon you can see all the stars.

Desdemona

It sure is Iago, and my kind of man saying that.
Whispering then Kisses him

Iago

I did not know you had a crush on me, I have known you when you were that tall
He acts like when since she was a child.

Desdemona

Your so authoritative, so decisive. You want some wine or more pasta.

Iago

Some wine would be fine.
She pours some more wine in his glass.
So how long have you had this crush on me

Desdemona

Since I was about 13
If I was the prize in a jousting tournament would you enter.

Iago

I would and win

Desdemona

Then I will ask to be given away to the tournament hoping you will win.
You will be my champion.
A most fitting husband to be.
Get married in the cathedral.

Iago

After what I saw with Othello, I will be your champion.
Bowing
Its late I must get home I have to train my men in the morning.
Iago gives Desdemona a kiss and a hug
Do you want a escort home?

Desdemona

Yes I will take you up on that.
Yells
Bye Peril
They both leave

Peril

Bye Desdemona, see you tomorrow.
Rodegro your not going anywhere.
Takes his hand leads him to the bedroom turns out candle.

room gets dark. What happens next is the audiences imagination.
Next morning

Rodegro
In bed
I must get up dear and get to the blacksmith and overlook the job making the armor for the horses

Peril
You welcome to come tonight.

Rodegro
If I am done with my task you will see me.
gets up and proceeds to exit the villa
Seine changes to the blacksmith forge.
Forges were the industry of the city, and blacksmiths used them to make weapons armor what ever they needed for combat.
Catapracts used Clydesdales that could take a tremendous amount of weight.
Getting enough Clydesdales is going to be a challenge if Computer animation is not used. It will result in some spectacular scenes.

Rodegro
Walks in blacksmith
Is the horses plate mail done?
He inspects the plate mail
he gets upset
This Plate mail is too thin it has to be able to stop a hand cannon shot.

Blacksmith
It will make the cost of each horse double in price for the armor.

Rodegro
Its better than an
a dead Catapract. Make them to my specifications. Do not deviate from them.

Blacksmith
Shaking his head
Yes sir I will do my best.
Changes the seine to Barbantio overlooking the construction of the walls and keeps.

Barbantio
To construction crew
Let me remind you men we are taking on a foe that uses only gunpowder. We must make our walls thick enough to take a considerable force from cannons.

Lead Forman
Yes sir.

Look of ramps and pulleys making the walls of the city.
Sir the castle in that backs up the south wall on the hill is done.

Barbantio

Message Sir Ruth that the castle for the colossus cannon is done and have it transported to the defensive position.

Lead Forman

Will do Sir

Barbantio

Inspects keep behind south wall.
Men your building the most important defense building on the south wall.

One of the men

Yes Sir.

Barbantio

You better, I am going to be in it.
Points at it.
The Keep is just behind the south wall
Change of seine again to Iago drilling swordsmen

Duke of Venice

How is the training going Iago
Sound of sword fighting

Iago

They are second to none if our walls are breached.
I hope they are not used.

Duke of Venice

Walls no matter how thick you make them do not resist cannon fire very long it is to slow them down that is about it.
You may be the ones that take out the last of the Janssarys you will never know.
The best we can do is be prepared for the attack.
Scene changes to Cassio's crew drilling for the Turkish fleet attack.

Cassio

On the Flying Dragon
From what the duke said, we are going to be out numbered.

Ruth

I be at your back dear making sure nothing happens to you!

Cassio

We may be boarded this time Ruth.

Ruth

They would wish they did not on my ship.
I will guard the shore and do my best they do not get on shore.
If I am sunk I will head for the castle if not captured.

Casanova

Rack, Right toots
Ruth goes to the Desdemona by row boat

Cassio

Men lets drill for getting prepared for battle.

Mr Chiristanson

Get prepared for battle

Second mate

Eye Sir.
They all rush to battle stations.

Mr Chiristanson

Ready for fire blast.

Second mate

Eye Sir

Mr Chiristanson

Message Ruth the Castle is ready for the cannon

Second mate

Eye sir
Aboard Desdemona

Ruth

We must unload the cannon to be taken to the castle make way to port.

Mr Romero

Eye Mam

Scene IV
Battle of Venice (The events to the actual land battle)

This is were we part the Red Sea. In my story I have as much as eight dialogs going at once here it is not going to be different. Director may have to show scenes in rapid succession. Overlapping dialog may be needed. This is where the grand spectacle that makes it my work comes out. Hopefully not too much on the producers pocket book too.
"This is better than any Tempest storm"
Use computer animation when needed
Aboard the Flying Viking

Second mate
In crows nest,
Sir I count ten ships to the port bow maybe more

Mr Christanson
Message the rest of our fleet.

Cassio
Prepare our fast rigging for hit and run tactics. Send one of our brigs back to Venice to notify Iago.
The Turks are within three hours getting near Venice.
The Desdemona is near shore with three brigs near Venice
Signal all our fire ships for battle.
Attack the transports first priority.

Turkish Captains
First ship **Fire**
Second ship

Fire
Directors discretion if he or she wants more.
Turkish fire over shoots the fire ships again

Cassio
Signal ships stay away from broad sides. Attack the sterns of ships

Mr Christanson
Eye Sir
Prepare for fire blast
Make sure ballast's are secured.

Second mate
Eye sir.

300 meters…
100 Meters

Cassio
Fire

Second fire ship
Fire

Third fire ship
Fire.
There is fire spewing everywhere cannons making splashes all over the place.
One of the transports blows up the concussion is almost defining.
Second transport the rigging is on fire the third the helm.

Cassio
Disengage the enemy Mr Christanson

Mr Christanson
We have them on the run.

Cassio
I said, Make it so.
The Byzantine ships disengage the enemy,
one ship is hit by cannon fire hitting their rigging. Show their mast falling
Message the damaged ship fight on to the death. Do not surrender.

Mr Christanson
Eye sir.
Disabled ship still keeps firing till they are out of Greek fire.
Takes several hits by cannon fire the ship starts taking on water.
Two of the Turkish ships is entirely engulfed with flames.
The third has a helm that is not useable.
They are abandoning ship.
Men aboard the Flying Dragon cheer for their fellow seamen.

Seamen of the Flying Dragon
Yeh!

Cassio
If your going to down take two or three with you

Mr Christanson
Smiles, I agree sir

Second mate
Three ships pursuing us. Breaking off from the fleet.

111

Cassio

Turn to attack

Attack the perusing ships

The Byzantine ships make a fast 180 turn

they attack the three ships that left the Turkish fleet They are totally engulfed in fireballs that the

cannons are too hot to touch.

One blows up

Cassio

Proceed to attack the fleet again

Mr Christanson

That's if we can catch them

Cassio

We do not have tons of cargo like they do

Mr Christanson

That's true sir.

Second mate

Three transports port bow!

Cassio

Prepare to engage the enemy.

Mr Christanson

eye sir

Scene shows them attacking the transports the Colossus one blows up

Aboard the Desdemona it has just delivered Cannon on shore to be taken to the castle.

Second mate

in Crows nest yelling

One Brig dead ahead. They are signaling us mam *pause*

Turkish fleet behind them.

Ruth

Signal the rest of our ships be prepared for battle.

Get secure our ballast and get ready for fire blast.

Mr Romero

Eye Mam

Ruth

Guard our shore we are to take out as many ships we can. Signal on land the Turkish Fleet is

within two hours of shore.

Mr Romero

eye mam

Ruth

prepare the life boats for fast exit. The odds we are facing we may not have a ship under us.

Mr Romero

I bet we take a lot with us though.

Ruth

It may be a exit with lots of pizzazz.

Mr Romero

A fast one at that too Mam

The message brig joins Ruth for defense of the shoreline.
Turkish Fleet starts firing at Ruth's ships

Ruth

Attack their stern Mr Romero Stay away from their broadsides.
Fire blast at their rigging.

Mr Romero

Eye mam.

The Desdemona and the other ships attack the Turkish fleet.
The Desdemona causes the first Turks rigging on fire. Turns again to the second ship puts their rigging on fire. The brigs cannons are firing at the bigger Turkish ships there are cannon splashes everywhere.
One of the brigs are taking on water fast they abandon ship.
The Desdemona takes on a third ship one of the ships rigging that was on fire explodes.

Ruth

Cover our men that are abandoning that brig.

On shore is the horse to take Ruth to the castle long shot of the battle from shore
The Desdemona is taking on a fourth ship it is hit by cannon fire but causes the ships rigging to catch fire.

Mr Romero

We are taking on water fast mam

Ruth

Fire on that ship and then abandon ship

Mr Romero

Eye mam We can not fire on them when the water gets past our Greek fire.

Ruth

Fire on them as long as we can.

The fourth ships rigging is set fire and they are abandoning ship

113

Mr Romero

We can not fire on them anymore mam
Seines the ship taking on water fast

Ruth

No use staying here and be boarded abandon ship

Mr Romero

ABANDON SHIP
Ruth gets into life boat and as many crew man as well to row to shore, Casanova is on her shoulder.
Cannon splashes everywhere
Scene changes to them close to shore.
They all exit the rowboat. Shows the fleet behind them brigs are still firing at the Turks.
Ruth gets wet and ties her shirt around her breasts she exits the row boat and gets on shore all wet. The
scene must be very sexy. The horses to take them to the castle is waiting for them. Cannon
wising fire hitting the shore.
She gets on the horse and rides to the castle
where the colossus cannon is.

Ruth

Mr Romero catch up with me at the castle to be ready to man the cannon.
She rides off to castle

Mr Romero

Will Do Mam
Scenes of her on horseback directors discretion.
At castle

Ruth

To second mate
Is the cannon ready?

Second Mate

Yes mam all hell is ready to rain upon them.
Scenes of the Turks landing and showing many tents of the army.
Night fall and changes seine to Barbantio's keep.

Barbantio

To Iago
Looks like the Turks are making camp tonight. They lost about 1000 men from are navy. Tell the
men to be ready for attack in the morning

Iago

I will notify Rodegro to make Calvery raids Tonight.
Seine changes to Iago chatting with Rodegro base of Barbantio's keep.

Rodegro is on horse
Peril is sees Rodegro
Rodegro the Turks are making camp do what you can sabotage and
capture as much artillery you can..

Peril
Be careful Rodegro
He gets off his horse they kiss and a hug. Then gets back on his Catapract rides to his men. Directs them
to follow him.
They get closer to the Turkish camp and they hear belly dancing music.
The Turks are having a pep rally. All the Turks are watching six belly dancers and they are mesmerized
what is happening around them. They are crowded around them Show the dancing for a few minutes.

Rodegro
Gets off his horse at a good viewing point without being seen.
looks in his glass Sees the belly dancers have the Turks attention. Then he sees the horses and cannons.
To his second in command Mr. Richardson
Looks like we are going to steal some cannons and horses tonight.

Mr. Richardson
Next to Rodegro
Sounds good sir and we have a great diversion.

Rodegro
Chuckles ... Those belly dancers may very well help us win the battle tomorrow.
They proceed quietly to steal the horses and cannons They steal all but six that are locked in their
positions
A guard sees them shoots his hand cannon, but the music is so loud the rest of them can not hear it. He
is Cut down by one of the Catapracts. The shot from the hand cannon bounces off the Catapracts.
Directors dispersion the music.
He quietly signals to get out of there they are taking cannons and horses.
They hear hand cannon shots in the distance. Sound of whizzing shot.
They approach their fortifications.

Ralph the gate keeper
Who goes there

Rodegro
Ralph you know who I am let us in.

Ralph the Gate keeper
Barbantio told me do not let anyone in without the pass word.
What is the password?

Rodegro
Ralph do I have a Janessary domed helmet on? Do I look like a Turk?
Let me in or I will have you whipped. and dragged across Venice!

Ralph the gate keeper
Yes sir, OPEN THE GATE!
They enter the fortifications
Seines of the Byzantine setting up captured cannons

Scene V
The Land battle

Next morning at dawn the Turkish camp

Turkish Engineer.
Looking for the keys to the locks to the cannons.
In Turkish
Those Byzantine swine they took our keys to the cannons. *In anger he shoots with a Six hand cannons the locks off the cannons so they can set them up that morning.*
Seines showing the Turkish drummers and trumpets. The sound of the drums and trumpets during the pending siege of the fortifications.
The 5000 Janessarys in rows with their domed helmets Marching, holding hand cannons. The remaining cannons that are being loaded to fire.
Director if possible Overlapping dialog.

Barbantio
At his Keep
Message all positions be ready for the impending attack.
The Turkish cannons open fire on the south wall,
Message Iago have his men be placed behind the south wall.
Captured cannons fire on the Janessary's

Ruth
Fire on those Janessarys. *With Casanova on her shoulder.*
The colossus cannon fires on the Janessarys takes out ten men.

Casanova
Rack, Enemy on port bow
Rack , Attack, Attack
Scene changes to Rodregro's attack at the Janessarys. The gleaming armor on the Catapracts as they charge the enemy swords swinging.

116

Rodegro

Charge! *The ground is rumbling from the 1500 heavy Catapracts they take on the front rows of Janessarys in a heated battle they kill at least 1000. Much of them are simply run over from the armored Clydesdales horses charge being trampled to death. They withdraw to attack the Cannons. They re group and get ready for another attack.*

Ruth

Such a pretty sight. It was all worth the effort. Fire on those positions *a big blast of the colossus cannon that hits the rear Janessarys this time twenty are killed.*

Casanova
Rack, Attack, attack
As the Janessarys get close to the walls the captured cannons open up on the marching troops.

1ˢᵗ Byzantine Cannons
Fire

2ⁿᵈ Byzantine cannons
Fire

3ʳᵈ Byzantine cannons
Fire

Greek Fire
fire
More directors discretion
Several positions different scenes

Barbantio
Commence fire!

Turkish officer
Fire
Mass shot hits the center of the South wall where Barbantio's keep is just behind. with devastating results.
Pieces of wall falling off.

The right Byzantine officer
Fire

The Left Byzantine Officer
Fire

Officer in castle

Fire

Arrows are raining down on the Janessarys that do not have shields. The sky is just filled with arrows that are about to hit the Janessarys many of them are killed by the arrows.

Six Turkish artillery

They fire on the same spot where the first volley of Janessarys hit and make a small hole in the wall six feet wide.

Janessarys start to go threw the wall with arrows raining down on them

Iago

To champion swordsmen and Greek Fire

Charge! *they immediately plug the hole skewering the charging Janessarys.*

Rodrego

Charge! *The Catapracts take to the field again this time they take out the cannons that breached the wall. With the sound of the ground rumbling the 1400 strong charge the enemy.* Charge those men! *They after attack the rear of the Janessarys trampling hundreds. Making them mass confusion the ranks break up.*

The shot from the Janessarys just bounce off the armor of the Catapracts. A few are killed but they have devastating attacks on the enemy.

Janessary officer

Fire! *as he points to Barbantio's keep hundreds of shot fire upon his keep and it the top of the keep is destroyed Barbantio is thrown from the keep and is instantly killed.*

Desdemona

She sees her father thrown from the keep

she runs to him and is crying is over her fathers body in tears.

Father, not like this!

Iago

sees she is in danger and kills a Janessary that is about to kill Desdemona

Get in the castle dear! *Drags her away from her fathers body. They take Barbantio in the castle as well.*

They keep firing cross bows after the Catapracts charge eventually all of them are killed. Iago's swordsmen kill the remaining Janessary's that made it threw the wall.

Ruth

Fires the cannon. That's for the ships you sunk! *Fist showing Thirty men are killed that time as they are very close.*

Casanova

RACK, Men on Deck, Men on Deck

In the castle Desdemona is kneeled by her father crying. Barbantio has blood all over from the shot and the destruction of the keep.

Duke of Venice
he try's to comfort Desdemona, holding her.
Your father fought with honor and with distinction to his position.
We will honor your father. He is the hero of the city we will never forget that.
We will construct a monument in his honor in the Venice square.

Iago
Iago comes In the room
To Desdemona
We have won the battle! Not one Turkish Soldier is alive thanks to your father.
He embraces Desdemona with a kiss as she still is in tears.
Scenes of the dead with the playing of green sleeves the women crying over dead Byzantine men, The battlefield, countless enemy dead are lying.
Seines of the belly dancers crying over the Turkish dead. (optional)
Scavengers are going over the bodies of the enemy.

Act IV
Scene I

The international Jousting tournament. and wedding.
Iago has a meeting with the Duke.

Iago
We should commence construction of the monument of Barbantio immediately.

Duke of Venice
Any suggestions what we are to make it of.
I am for a Marble statue.

Iago
Bronze is nice, But we have to import the materials. Marble we have plenty of.

Duke Of Venice
Marble it is and he will be buried with full honors in the Venice square. As soon as the Monument is constructed.

Iago
Sir, I was thinking being we won the battle lets put on a international jousting tournament. Invite knights from just about all the countries we can think of.

Duke of Venice
I love that idea invite knights from all countries no matter what genre they are.

Iago
Chuckles, Including Ruth

Duke of Venice
Smiles, including Ruth.
He goes into his secretary's office.
I want you to make a invitation to all the countries we have relationships with even enemies. All knights we are having a International Jousting tournament. The first of the month without delay.

Duke's Secretary
Yes sir I will send them out immediately

Iago
Desdemona has mentioned to me she wants to be one of the prizes.

Duke of Venice
I have to speak with her before I do it;
When I speak with her about funeral arrangements.
Desdemona enters office.

Desdemona
Sir here are some official papers I found at the house.
They look like they were when my father was a senator
She gives them to him.

Duke of Venice
These are most helpful. Iago tells me you want to be one of the prizes for the jousting
Tournament.

Desdemona
Yes, providing he is entered.

Iago
Sir you can consider me as the first entry to the contest.
Bows

Desdemona
Then I ask to be one of the prizes

Duke of Venice
It is official you are one of the prizes for the Jousting tournament.
Iago and Desdemona leave the Dukes office
Desdemona takes Iago's arm they are walking

Desdemona

I want to thank you for saving my life in the battle. Will you stay with me tonight. You are welcome to stay at my house.
We can have dinner and enjoy each others company.

Iago

It will be a honor to stay with you that is the least I can do after the death of your father.

Desdemona

They are walking to her house they meet Cassio and Ruth on the street
Oh look there is Cassio and Ruth.

Iago

I wanted to commend you both on your excellent performance on the water. Ruth the expertise the way you, fired the Colossus cannon very impressive. The duke is holding a intentional jousting tournament the first of the month.

Cassio

Sounds like fun, Ruth now is your chance to put the men in their place..

Ruth

It was nothing, that cannon is what made the performance, I just aimed it.

Casanova

Rack, Hi Toots
With enthusiasm

Ruth

Oh how fun, lets enter Cassio, Where do we enter?

Iago

The dukes office, all the countries that we have diplomatic ties will be there.

Ruth

We are going to his office to enter, Then we are going house hunting.
We have to buy some plate mail too.

Cassio

Nice seeing you both. bye
Both couples continue walking

Desdemona

Nice seeing you too.
Oh look there is Peril and Rodegro
They walk up to them

Iago
We have good news Venice is holding a international Jousting tournament.

Rodegro
Sounds great where do we enter.

Desdemona
The dukes office.

Peril
We were heading that way we will stop in, and I will make sure Rodegro enters.

Rodegro
Sounds good.

Iago
Bye.

Rodegro
Good by sir.
Iago and Desdemona continue down the street.
The five witches approach them looking for a Caldron for their spells.

Andrella
The five witches have been wandering the streets of Venice for weeks looking for a Caldron.
To Desdemona
Excuse me do you know where we can find a Caldron for us to make spells to get home.

Desdemona
My father has one from the Crusades. It is mine now.
She pulls Iago so the witches can not hear them.
Whispering to Iago. Remember what I told you about the Dread Black Knight of Masadonia.
He is going to be there for sure, once he gets word of the tournament.
They can keep him from getting to Venice.
To witches
Meet me at this address at noon and we will discuss you getting your caldron.
I am Desdemona your name is.

Andrella
I am Andrella this is Barbella, Lizzy, Tizzy, and Dizzy.
We are so happy to find a caldron; we have been looking for one for weeks. We will see you tomorrow at noon.
Both Iago and Desdemona finally get to her house. They walk in the house.

Iago

We met our share of people today

Desdemona

The witches seamed to be nice, you want some pasta.
I have some shrimp does that sound good.
We have wine too.

Iago

That sounds good. So how do you think they can keep him from coming.

Desdemona

If they can take the handkerchief off of Othello they can do anything. They knew it is magical
just by looking at it.
Did you notice it was Othello's handkerchief on Lizzy she was wearing it. It had my perfume on it.
He opens the wine and pours it. They sit down at the table. They eat dinner.

Iago

So are you going to ask them to turn him into a toad.

Desdemona

He has a crush on me. I would not ask that, just that he does not get to Venice for the tournament
and we are married. It does not matter anymore when we are married.

Iago

He still will be out there with the feelings for you.

Desdemona

What matters we are together that is what matters. I will never know how its like to be with him.
He respects my feelings and does not want to hurt me. HE will not come once we are married.

Iago

There is the chance I can be beaten.

Desdemona

You are my champion and protector you already have demonstrated that.
I would not give myself to the tournament if I had doubts, and put my self as the prize.

Iago

I am happy you have such faith in me.
he kisses her hand.

Desdemona

Desdemona is the one that gets the ideas that are the plot in the story.
You know would it be grand if we have a triple wedding in the Venice Cathedral after the
Tournament.

You, Me, Cassio, Ruth, Peril, and Rodegro.

Iago

I like that Idea, A toast to the wedding of the century *They toast to the idea.*

Desdemona

First you must win the tournament. My father would want it that way.
Iago gets up takes her hand and they slow dance

Iago

There is a row boat the moon is full lets go out on the lake.

Desdemona

Lets go
Directors discretion
They dance some more then they go to the lake.
She takes off her shoes and gets into the row boat Iago
rows out to the middle with the moon shimmering on the lake.

Iago

The lake looks Beautiful with the full moon on the lake.

Desdemona

Yes it does with you in the boat makes all the better. Oh look the swans in the water so
magnificent aren't they. You know they mate for life. That is what I want.

Iago

Rowing
So it shall be, Their life is much shorter than ours though.

Desdemona

Still even if we disagree it is worth it.

Iago

Sometimes is OK, All the time is not so nice.

Desdemona

In good times and bad they have to live threw them as a team.

Iago

Long as they think in terms of we than me, we are OK.

Desdemona

Once we are married I will work hard to not think of just myself. I will think of what is good for
both of us not just me.

Iago

I will remind you of that

Desdemona

We both work on that. Good communication is important too.
If I knew that Othello was using magic on me I would
never have married him.
He deceived me and he was a fraud.
Honesty and integrity. It is best we don't keep secrets that would spoil our marriage.

Iago

Honesty and integrity is the only way to be with us.
Aren't we a little a head of our selves.

Desdemona

Not really nothing wrong with thinking about it.
Nether person has it over the other.
Win, win relationship

Iago

I agree.
They both lie side by side in the row boat
Iago puts his fingers threw Desdemona's hair and kissing her passionately
She kisses him all over
Directors discretion this scene Romantic kissing hugging
The camera makes a long shot they fall asleep on the row boat and wake up when the boat is hitting the
shore in the morning.
Peril is passing Desdemona's house
Peril sees them in the boat and throws some fruit to wake them up.
Desdemona is startled by the fruit hitting her chest.

Peril

Good Morning , you two have been out their all night.

Desdemona

giggling yes we have
she gets out of the boat stumbles gets her blouse wet and splashes water on Iago
Get up silly, it's morning

Iago

Gets out and splashes her back.
Then they hug and kiss each other.
Good morning dear

Peril

I will see you later. *Throws another fruit to Iago he catches it*
Walks down the street.

Bye

Iago
I must go, I have pressing matters for work
Bye peril thanks for the Fruit
waves to Peril

Desdemona
Bye Peril see you later
I have my meeting with the witches soon
Iago walks to work.
Desdemona goes inside the villa and cleans up from the evening.
AS soon as she gets done two puffs of smoke appear at the door one green the other white. She comes to the door
Your here early.

Andrella
All we were thinking last night is the hope to get home. We want to see the Caldron you were talking about

Desdemona
She takes them outside in the back and shows them a caldron three foot high and just as much in diameter
My father used it for feeding the crusaders.

Andrella
What do you think Dizzy?

Dizzy
I can reverse the spell with this for sure,
and what ever else you want.

Andrella
So what do you want from us?
Desdemona gets goes inside and they follow.

Desdemona
The first if the month Venice is holding a international jousting tournament.
There is this knight he is the dread Black Knight of Masadonia
that has had a crush on me since I was 13 and I am the prize for the tournament.
What I want from you all is to keep him from getting to Venice without turning him into a toad.

Andrella
What route is he taking?

Desdemona

The only route from Masadonia goes threw the black forest of thorns. I will mark it on this map.

She gives the map to her.
All the witches huddle
Whispering

Dizzy

Lets do it, should not be too hard to detour one knight.

They break the huddle

Andrella

WE will do it then, we get the caldron

Desdemona

YES defiantly

He is not just any knight he a most formidable knight he has killed over 250 men.

You must be careful to stay out of sight.

Andrella

I hear that forest is magical, we will make a point to not be seen.

She shakes Desdemona's hand.

You have a deal, that knight will not be in Venice ever.

Desdemona

I will have your caldron ready and cleaned; it will be ready when your done with your quest.

Shows them outside of the house.

Bye and good luck., Be careful that man is very dangerous.

Andrella

Bye Desdemona

Seine II
Forest of Thorns.

The set is as gruesome as possible. forest trees all have thorns. One week later the five witches get to the location were the dread Black Knight of Masadonia will be traveling threw. Computer animation growth of the forest and petrifaction.

Andrella

I am open for ideas, sure is a gruesome place

William Quayle Jr.

Lizzy
I'd start using these trees; I can make a spell they move and knock him off his horse.

Tizzy
Then the trees attack him, anything else he would kill. Have the trees block is path to the city so they are so thick he can not pass.

Dizzy
I can make a dragon

Andrella
He would just kill it and keep going.
I like the idea forces of nature.
After he falls off his horse the trees grow all around him so he can not move.
Make the growing forest petrified so he can not cut his way out of the thick forest.
We make spells around him to keep him from being mobile.

Barbella
I am good at making trees move.

Dizzy
I am good making trees grow.

Tizzy
I can make the trees move too

Lizzy
I will make the forest petrified once they grow.

Andrella
I will help you Lizzy
Well we have our plan lady's lets find that black Knight
They see a dark figure in the distance in the shape of a horseman.

Tizzy
Looks like we have our Knight

Dizzy
I agree

Tizzy and Barbella
Forces of nature day and night, make the trees in flight, strike that Knight.
Once, twice three times their branches flowing with a striking blow.
A magical flash three trees move toward the Knight and turn their branches and strike him off his horse. Computer animation.

Andrella
whispering thumbs up
Well done Tizzy and Barbella
The black knight gets up looks for his horse.

Dizzy
Post haste trees grow, Make them Flow, All around him not able to mow.
Flash of light
The trees rapidly grow around the knight with thorns he is stuck in one spot he gets out his ax starts chopping the trees.

Andrella
Thumbs up to Dizzy

Lizzy and Andrella
Land, water fire, make the forest the rock of ages,
Surround our subject with reckless rage.
May the forest forever petrified with no age.
May imprison him in a timeless cage.
He breaks his ax on the trees
Thunder and lighting the forest all around the Black Knight is surrounding him in petrified forest. He can not move or cut the forest he is trapped in their spell until they release him.

Andrella
Lets get out of here.

Seine II

The five witches find their way home
They knock on Desdemona's door
She answers the door

Desdemona
Welcome back I have your caldron ready. How did it go.

Andrella
Well you will find he will not bother you till your married.
He is imprisoned in a petrified forest of thorns.
We knew he would win physical conflict anything we made.
We just accelerated Nature.
The spell will be broken once your married

Lizzy
More like a rampage!

Barbella
We did not put spells on him directly, just all around him

Dizzy
Well I better get started to reverse my spell.
Might as well do it here if that's ok.

Desdemona
That's fine with me, I like to see you get home.

Tizzy
We have to go out and gather the things for the caldron we will be back.
They all leave
seines gathering everything Fast
then show them coming back.

Dizzy
We have everything we need for our travel back to our homes.
Our chicken
are you good making chicken
We only need the foot.

Desdemona
Guess I can put it in my pasta
This is like getting ready for a Mid evil space voyage.
It is like ET going home, only its the 13th century.

Lizzy
lets make double sure so we don't end up in a place like China or the North pole.
Oak tree root

Tizzy
she is checking the list
check

Lizzy
Snake tail

Tizzy
Check

Lizzy
eagles egg

Tizzy
Check

Lizzy
Black widow spider

Tizzy
Check

Lizzy
Bats wing

Tizzy
check

Dizzy
ONE CHICKENS FOOT

Tizzy
Your making double sure this time!
CHECK!

Dizzy
we let it boil up for two hours.

Desdemona
The chicken pasta is ready.

Barbella
Lets Eat
They all eat dinner then go back to the Caldron

Dizzy
The caldron is ready!

Andrella
Dizzy no be careful with your words to your spell

Dizzy
London, Ozone way we go
May we go home, make it so.
All powerful magic make it flow.
In a pouf of smoke make it glow.
Her wand touches the Caldron
makes a green and white pouf of smoke all five disappear.
Directors discretion showing them home.
Some computer animation would be cool then showing them home

It would make a emotional moment for the audience.

Desdemona
She claps her hands
I wonder if they made it. *looking up in night sky.*
sits on balcony love seat
She sees some green and white streaks in the night sky.
She smiles and a emotional gesture,
and goes to bed.

Seine III

The Barbantio Memorial and
International Jousting Tournament.
Shows Desdemona in a black gown
on the deck of the Government building
The monument of Barbantio is to be unveiled.
The Duke of Venice to give a speech.
Huge crowd in Venice square.

Duke of Venice
Inspirational music in background.
To crowd in square.
Citizens of Venice we are gathered her today to pay tribute to a true hero of Venice.
I man that dedicated his life as a knight and a senator of our fair city.
When we were participating in the Crusades he represented us with honor.
When our city was at war with the Turks he again offered his services the Defender of Venice. He designed formidable defenses for our city. Enlisted and trained a formidable force to defend our city. He gave his life defending us.
I therefore dedicate this memorial to our hero.
Barbantio the Defender of Venice!
Long to a close shot showing marble statue of Barbantio in crusades armor applause of the crowd.
They unveil his memorial
The duke sits down and
Desdemona addresses the crowd.

Desdemona
from balcony
We are here today to honor my father, a man of honor and distinction.
When I was deceived, he defended my honor.
When the situation looked like we were alone against the Turks. He was a leader and we followed him to our victory, to defend our city so we can live in freedom.
Venice we are going to celebrate our victory by having a international Jousting tournament.

From this moment I formally announce the Venice international jousting tournament is has commenced.

Knights from 14 countries are entered men and woman can compete in the same arena. Officially we have entries from Britain, France, Holy Roman Empire, Moorish Empire, Masadonia, Even our enemy the Turkish empire is entered, China, Japan, India, Arabia, Persia, Egypt, and Denmark.

The events are in three categories:

Saber without armor.

Combat with full armor.

Calvery combat.

Venue is flexible change seine to action fast.

Desdemona and Peril in stands

Show the arena and the combat starting.

Directors discretion all combat. a lot of clanking of armor, shields keep the audience on the edge.

Director must have experience in Melee fighting.

Ruth kisses Cassio

Cassio

Be careful dear *Kisses her*

Ruth

No problem, least there is only one.

Announcer

The rules, no killing in this contest, once a competitor is down and yields the contest is over.

The first contest is saber without armor.

The British entry

Sir Randolph Scott;

the Byzantine entry;

Sir Ruth the Admiral

Ruth is dressed in a loose blouse

Sir Randolph Scott

Now I get to skewer you for ran sacking Nassau.

Sir Ruth

she slices his shirt

You were saying. I could have killed you.

They have a heated fight

They fight until he is on the ground and he yields.

Not all women have to wear dresses.

Sir Randolph Scott is mad he got beat by a woman he is cussing like crazy

Sir Randolph Scott

That woman is a witch, You hear me she is a witch, I tell you

Pointing at her

Ruth
Yelling back at him
You British call all woman that wear pants witches, I'm just a better swordsman than you.
Crowd cheers. She bows
Cassio is laughing on sidelines.
The Duke is laughing next to him.
Ruth's men are laughing too

Peril
Kisses Rodrego on horse
Run him in the ground sweety
Good luck

Announcer
The second contest is Calvery combat
The Byzantine entry
Sir Rodrego
The French entry
Sir Lafeate Perre
the ribbon is dropped both full speed toward each other
Rodegro hits the Frenchman's horse with his lance and the horse bolts backward the French entry is thrown from his horse.
He gets off his horse and pulls out his ax. He breaks it on the third blow. The Frenchman takes out his ax and throws it at him. He misses he pulls out his broadsword and they fight until the Sir Lafeate Perrie yields. Rodegro bows The Frenchman shakes his hand. and bows too.

Iago
To Desdemona
I have to fight Othello's brother coming up

Desdemona
You will do fine, he is not as fast as his brother was.
Do not try to over power him though he is very strong. Make your blows count.
She kisses him
Fight on my champion!
he goes in the arena
Iago
He is fighting with his broadsword he has his ax on his back

Announcer
Our third event is
Combat with full armor.
Byzantine entry
Sir Iago
The Moor entry
Sir Mobello
The both get in arena a start combat

Iago is suppose to win so the director is to make it look good yet real. Lot of clanking and swords hitting each other. Mobello trying to over power him Iago maneuvers with from his blows. Mobello is knocked to the ground and yields.
Have some close calls too.
Iago wins and bows
Mobello shakes hands with him.

Mobello
Smiles, Good fight, It is good to see you sir.
The tournament can be a movie in it self we go straight to the finals we are going to be at the maximum time with what we have.

Announcer
We are down to the final six entries.
We will have the final of the Saber
Competition.
Of the Byzantine Empire
Sir Ruth
The Japanese Empire
Sir Yamamoto
heated melee conflict for five minutes clanking of swords really fast. the Japanese slices Ruth's shirt she is all over the arena
Ruth makes a brilliant charge on Sir Yamamoto.
He gets on his heals and stumbles he goes across the area in defense of Ruth's speed with a sword then he falls and yields in a very aggressive attack.
Ruth helps him up.
He bows and shakes her hand
The crowd cheers she goes to the award stand the Duke gives her trophy and gets a big hug and a kiss from Cassio. Then she walks around the arena showing her trophy with hugs from her crewmen.

Announcer
Now the final for the
Calvery combat.
For the Byzantine Empire
Sir Rodegro
For the Holy Roman Empire
Sir Hans Robeck
The ribbon drops
They both bolt fast to each other
Rodegro makes a solid hit but does not
make him budge
They make runs to each other three times the fourth
Rodegro
hits his horse and his horse bolts backward.
The both get off their horses have a heated battle
Rodegro eventually wins.
Directors discretion

*Rodegro gets back on his horse goes over to stands where Peril is
and pulls her up behind him they ride his horse around the arena
With a emotional response to the crowd.*

Desdemona
To Iago
Concentrate make your bows count.
Fight on my Champion!
She kisses him
Iago goes into arena
Announcer
Next is the Combat with Armor
for the Byzantine Empire
Sir Iago
For the Chinese Empire
Sir Hag So Ping
Ribbon drops
*Sir Hag So Ping is using a spike mace and is making a aggressive attack on Iago making him deflect
with his shield, moving Iago back.
Iago hustles to keep on his feet.
He makes a fast move and strikes with his sword Sir Hag So Pings back
making him stumble forward.
Directors discretion the rest of the battle.
Iago after falling gets back up and makes blows that puts his opponent down and he yields.
Iago helps him up Sir Hag So Ping shakes his hand.*

Announcer
Sir Rodegro and Sir Iago and Sir Ruth
have won the tournament
Peril has Sir Rodegro hand or was that the other way around.
Desdemona Sir Iago has her hand
May I present our winners of the tournament.
Ruth, Cassio, Peril , Rodegro, Desdemona and Iago
It is almost sundown

Ruth
How did you win Cassio
Cassio
I have you that is all that matters. The crowd has their heroes.
He kisses her.
Night fall and there is a fireworks display

Ruth
LOOK Cassio Fireworks. She gives him a big hug

Cassio
The Chinese for their entry brought fireworks in goodwill.

He pulls her behind the stands.
And proposes to Ruth

Cassio
Ruth will you marry me.
They both have a very romantic kiss.

Ruth
YES, YES, YES
Ruth and Cassio runs to Desdemona, Iago, Peril and Rodegro that are together.

Ruth and Cassio
WERE GETTING MARRIED!

Cassio
Let celebrate and go to the Merchant of Venice

Desdemona, Iago, Peril and Rodegro
Lets go.
The merchant of Venice is a bar/pub whatever, and has most unusual entertainment.
It is a high class establishment
The belly dancers from before the battle are now dancing there.
They all sit down
Rodegro is laughing because of the belly dancers
belly dancing music in background.

Rodegro
I never think they be in here. They are nice to watch though.
Peril elbows him

Bar maid
Can I take your order**.**

Cassio
Your best wine for all of us.
Bar maid goes and brings their drinks
They are drinking wine.

Desdemona
I was mentioning to Iago before the tournament.

Peril
What is it Desdemona

Ruth
What is it.

Desdemona

The wedding of the Century all of us get married in the Cathedral. A Triple wedding. My father would want it that way.

Rodegro

That's a great Idea

Cassio

I agree

Ruth

We can start it with a bang.

Iago

Propose a toast to the wedding of the century.
They all give a hardy toast to their wedding.

Ruth

Can you imagine six cannons blasting away including the colossus cannon the exit of our wedding.

Desdemona

I like that.

Peril

Sounds great.

Iago

A toast to our Victory
They all toast.

Cassio

With all the planning you did Sir it is your victory. You have Desdemona too.

Ruth

I agree with Cassio it's Iago's Victory, we can celebrate tonight in freedom.
To our wedding.
She makes a toast.

All

To victory and our wedding

Casanova

Rack, bye, bye!

Epilog

The wedding of the century.
The Venice Cathedral

Venice was roman catholic at the time so they are having a roman catholic wedding.
It is the 14ᵗʰ century not the 21st. I am sorry if this offends peoples religion that is what was prevalent in Venice. Sighting Spirit of Barbantio optional.
This is concrete no exemptions short version of 1812 overture upon their exit. Cannons out side the Cathedral to fire with the music. 1812 overture should be timed upon their exit. The short version is 3.32 min long so the director should plan accordingly. Any other music before or after is OK.
Director is to make this short and emotional. If there is time for more then show the reception. If not leave like I have it.
All three couples are in front of Msr. Montebello
All three couples are in formal dress
directors discretion uniforms etc.
Skip the vows and go straight to the exit.   They take their time to line up to go down the isle. As the music tempo accelerates they rush out of the cathedral.

Msr Motebello
Ladies and gentlemen may I present the brides and grooms.
All three couples exit and go down the isle.
With the people invited clapping
1812 Overture Music starts. Cannons are ready to fire at the right time.
You show them outside then get a long shot.
Camera pans to outside all three brides with grooms throw their flowers. They get showered with rice then the camera pans the credits start. Camera shows a shot on the hill with the Dread Black Knight of Masadonia on the hill rearing his horse.
Casanova flies into view

Casanova
Rack, The End

Note: there is a lot of non dialog seines in this screenplay so I made room for them. Example the naval and land battles, the individual combat. I figure there is a good 55 minutes of action this screenplay.